Gentle Whispers

By
Catherine Grace

Gentle Whispers

Gentle Whispers

Copyrights © 2025 Catherine Grace All rights reserved.

No part of this publication may be reproduced, stored in a retrieval system, or transmitted in any form or by any means, electronic, mechanical, photocopying, recording, or otherwise, without prior written permission from the author, except in the case of brief quotations used in reviews or scholarly work.

Published in Australia by Sydney Book Publishers

Cover design and sketches by Catherine Grace

Edited by Sydney Book Publishers

Printed in Australia

Scripture taken from the HOLY BIBLE, NEW INTERNATIONAL VERSION R, NIV R. Copyright © 1973, 1978, 1984 by International Bible Society. Used by permission. All rights reserved worldwide.

Scripture taken from THE MESSAGE Copyright © 1993,1994,1995,1996,2000.2001,2002. Used by permission of NavPress Publishing Group.

Scripture taken from NEW LIVING TRANSLATION Copyright © 1996, 2004, 2015. Used by permission of Tyndale House Publishers.

Scripture taken from THE PASSION TRANSLATION © Used by permission of Passion & Fire Ministries Inc.

Scripture taken from GOOD NEWS TRANSLATION-Second Edition Copyright © 1992 by American Bible Society. Used by permission.

Scripture taken from NEW KING JAMES VERSION ® Copyright © 1982 by Thomas Nelson. Used by permission.

Please note that some names and identifying details have been changed to protect the privacy of individuals

Catherine Grace

Dedication

To my precious three grandchildren – I am so grateful that your Mum and Dad have given me the most priceless gifts of 'you!' I cherish every memory you have given me throughout your young lives.

In the years to come, it is my deepest desire that you will always know that no matter how sad or bad the world seems, there is always enough beauty to be found, and that you will know this through the Gentle Whispers Jesus has prepared especially for you. What a privilege and joy it is to be doing life with you, and I can't wait to see the adventures that lie ahead.

Jesus said:

"Let the little children come to me,

Don't stop them!

For the Kingdom of Heaven

belongs to those who are

like these children."

Matthew 19:14 NLT

Gentle Whispers

Giving glory to God through sharing true stories that will bring light, love and a deeper understanding of how God desires to speak to His children.

C.S. Lewis once surmised –
"Each person is created to see a different facet
of God's beauty –
something no one else can see in quite
the same way,
and then to bless all worshippers through
all eternity with an aspect of God
they could not otherwise see."
C.S. Lewis 29.11.1988 – 29.11.1963

Publish His glorious deeds
among the nations.
Tell everyone about the
amazing things He does.
Psalm 96:3 NLT

Catherine Grace

Table of Content

Dedication iv
Beginnings 2
Chapter One When I Was Lost...10
Chapter Two Knock Knock! 22
Chapter Three: "I'm Sure You Can!"....................................32
Chapter Four: Love Is A Many Splendid Thing..................48
Chapter Five: Home Sweet Home 70
Chapter Six: Sounds of Goodbye...88
Chapter Seven: Why Are We Waiting? 104
Chapter Eight: Can You Hear Me?.....................................122
Chapter Nine: In The Wee Small Hours............................140
From Beginning To End...160
Appreciations 176
About The Author 178

Gentle Whispers

By
Catherine Grace

Gentle Whispers

Beginnings -
a very good place to start

Catherine Grace

Beginnings

After the wind

there was an earthquake...

After the earthquake

there was a fire...

But the Lord was not in the

wind, the earthquake or the fire.

But after the fire came a

Gentle Whisper.

From 1 Kings 19:11-12 NIV

Hello there. Well, who'd have thought it would be me again, writing my thoughts and stories for you all to be reading? It seems absolutely ages since I was sitting at the computer, tap tap tapping away, but these thoughts, like my previous book on beauty, just won't go away.

This time, though, it isn't homework for a writing course that has happened to find its way into bookshops, but a more purposeful 'me' planning for this book to be in your hands, warming your hearts, and hopefully bringing heaven a little closer through my considerations of Gentle Whispers.

I know my thoughts can sometimes be a little 'different' to everyone else's, but it's in sharing our differences that we can all grow and learn from each other. What a lovely notion. I was encouraged by these words I read recently:

"Each person is created to see a different facet of God's beauty, something no one else can see in quite the same way. It is then we are able to bless them with an aspect of God's beauty they could not otherwise see."

C. S. Lewis 29.11.1898 – 22.11.1963

Gentle Whispers

So here I am, not writing a fictional novel – which I was hoping I would do one day – but instead writing some thoughtful, inspirational true short stories from my life, about a subject that is very near to my heart.

It is with a little fear and trembling that I begin these true narratives, but I do hope they strike a chord and bring some light and love into your day. As you read on, I hope the different ways I see some concepts of life in this wide, wonderful, and sometimes complicated world of ours will bless you and help you to see things a little 'out of the box!'

Have you ever heard that 'still small voice' or had a thought you know you couldn't have made up on your own? Have you ever been part of an experience, or found yourself in circumstances, you knew couldn't be a coincidence?

Well, I don't believe in coincidences, actually. Between you and me, I believe them to be God's surprises. I'm sure you know what I mean – those special moments in time that take your breath away with their uniqueness, wonder, and confirmation, showing there must be a Higher Power out there somewhere, who's looking out for you, with His plans and purposes to be revealed.

I believe God is always working in our lives with things we could never do for ourselves; that's why these surprises often come in the form of Gentle Whispers. Some of these whispers are to bring joy to our day, but some also have a purpose to help someone else. If we trust Him to bring along these blessings, then I believe He will!

It is so comforting to remember that God also knows you so deeply, like no other. The little duck dance from your favourite feathered friend you encountered this morning on your daily walk – it was just for you! Who else would be as happy with such frivolity as you would be?

Have you ever heard a Gentle Whisper? I have never 'heard' an audible voice or whisper from God. Oh, how amazing would that be! But I am content with the thoughts and unique circumstances He brings to my days, that I know could only come from Him. I do know some very special people have heard God's voice throughout history, even children.

Catherine Grace

<u>The story of Eli and Samuel</u>

One night, Eli, whose eyes were becoming so weak that he could barely see, was lying down in his usual place. The lamp of God had not yet gone out, and Samuel was lying down in the house of the Lord, where the ark of God was. Then the Lord called Samuel.

Samuel answered, "Here I am." And he ran to Eli and said, "Here I am; you called me." But Eli said, "I did not call; go back and lie down."

Now Samuel did not yet know the Lord: the word of the Lord had not yet been revealed to him.

Samuel thought he heard Eli call him three times...

Then Eli realised that the Lord was calling the boy.

So Eli told Samuel, "Go and lie down, and if He calls you, say, 'Speak, Lord, for your servant is listening.'" So Samuel went and lay down in his place.

The Lord came and stood there, calling as at the other times, "Samuel! Samuel!"

Then Samuel said, "Speak, for your servant is listening."

And the Lord said to Samuel: "See, I am about to do something in Israel that will make the ears of everyone who hears about it tingle."

Samuel 3:1–11 NIV

I find this story very encouraging, knowing that our Almighty God would even speak to a small child who maybe doesn't even believe in Him yet, with such an important message for the whole country of Israel. God was obviously speaking to Samuel in a way that would not frighten him – yes, gentle – because I believe God **is** there, watching over us every minute of every day, and His ways are always so thoughtful and kind. Whispers, because from my own experiences, God is always so very loving and caring in how He responds to His children. He loves us all so much!

I am reminded of a little game I used to play with my children when they were tiny. We would take it in turns to lean our eyelashes onto each other's cheeks, then blink our eyes ever so softly to give a 'flutterby kiss'. Of course, you know that means 'butterfly', don't you? Well, this is what a Gentle Whisper can be like.

The whisper doesn't always have to be an audible sound. Often the whisper won't even be words. It can be a lovely gesture that crosses your path from a friend, or a prompting in your spirit to do something for someone else, showing us miracles are at work. Mind you, though, if you aren't listening, God can also be a big, booming voice, like a thunderous earthquake! Such are our rebellious, deaf ears sometimes!

The reassuring fact is, though, God is often the whisper after the big, booming noise, once He has our attention! Such is His ever-compassionate and considerate nature! I love what is written in the book of Job, a man who had many sufferings:

"And these are but the outer fringe of his works;

How faint the whisper we hear of Him!

Who then can understand the thunder of his power?"

Job 26:14

There was a time in my own life when I didn't think for a minute that the God of Heaven would have anything to say to little, insignificant me. If you have read my previous book *Beauty All Around*, you will know some of my very strict, religious background. The thought of God actually speaking to the people of this world was quite absurd and seemed disrespectful – even arrogant.

I have heard many stories of those who thought God was a huge, strict spiritual being who sat on His throne with a big stick, waiting for us to do something wrong! On the flip side of this, I have also been in churches where many of the speakers claim that God has told them many and varied things. I would sometimes shudder, wondering what God was thinking of all the things He was supposed to have told these people!

I am sometimes quite astounded when I hear people say, "God told me this" and "God told me that!" When I do hear it, I sometimes let my mind wander to the Heavenly realm, picturing an angel sitting next to

God saying, "Did you really say that?" I hope that isn't a tad too naughty!

In saying that, though, I am a believer that God does talk to those of His people who are willing to listen. Well, as I have experienced over the years, our loving Heavenly Father isn't the big boogie man who is waiting for us to fail at all. I have definitely learnt not to let any fundamental religious interpretation, or the eisegesis of some modern Pentecostalism use of the Word of God – the Bible – prevent me from hearing what God wants to say to me in whatever way He knows I can hear Him.

Each and every day, there are wonderful messages waiting for you to hear and experiences that will flood you with so much joy, love, and acceptance. Yes, you are important, and God has many surprises He can't wait to lavish upon you, and for you to pass onto others.

"My sheep hear my voice,

And I know them,

And they follow me."

John 10:27 NIV

One such whisper came my way as I was contemplating writing a second book. The sales of my first book were very encouraging, with only a few left, yet I wasn't convinced the thoughts I was having about writing *Gentle Whispers* were a book in the making! I wasn't really receiving any thoughts for a novel, so I went looking for the prophecy that was spoken over me when my first book was sitting on the computer as homework for a writing course. Ahhh yes, there it was:

"You have written a book.

You will write many books.

You will write under a different name.

It is time to stop hiding!"

Prophet Evangelist Ed Trout – Texas

Gentle Whispers

"You will write many books!" Why did I even doubt? Maybe it is something to do with my maiden name being 'Thomas', but yes, doubting I was! A few uncertain weeks passed, interrupted by life – oh, and Christmas, which is my most favourite time of year! I just adore turning our home into a wonderland of festive bling, believing Jesus' birthday is certainly worth celebrating in the most extravagant way.

Then the New Year came, with those thoughts starting again. I went to the computer to refresh my mind with what I had started to write earlier, and then the most beautiful Gentle Whisper came that I could ever have hoped for. It came in the form of a card from an encouraging friend. These were the words:

> *"Thanks for sharing God's love*
>
> *not only with your words*
>
> *but also with your life.*
>
> *Thanks for being who you are*
>
> *and doing what you do,*
>
> *you're appreciated more than you know."*

An unexpected card, penned by my Heavenly Father and delivered by His faithful child, who had no idea I needed this confirmation, and who had heard and acted on a Gentle Whisper! The Bible verse also in the card, found in 1 Peter 4:10 (TLB), says it so beautifully:

> *"God has given each of you*
>
> *some special abilities;*
>
> *Be sure to use them to help each other,*
>
> *passing on to others God's many*
>
> *kinds of blessings."*

Gentle Whispers certainly are a blessing. Oh, I am so excited about this journey we are beginning now. You may already be well on the way, but I do hope that through these simple and true stories, God will come a little closer and you will know, without a doubt, just how amazingly important, significant, and loved you are, as you experience the joy of Him speaking to you.

Yes, as you immerse yourself in the following pages, my prayer is that you will open your ears and heart to the wonders of 'Gentle Whispers!'

Gentle Whispers

Chapter One
When I Was Lost

"I've told you these things, to prepare you for rough times ahead." – John 16:1 – The Message

How many times have you heard your mother or father say those timeless, wise words, *"I have told you over and over again not to do that, or go there, or say that"*? From the time we are wee little babies, we are told what to do and what not to do. Isn't it interesting that the *nots* are always the things we tend to *do*? Even the Apostle Paul had his struggles, as we see when he said:

"I do not understand what I do. For what I want to do I do not do, but what I hate to do." – Romans 7:15 – NIV

Such is human nature and might I add, it's encouraging to know that an apostle who became a saint had the same struggles! On a daily basis we are continually fighting those *nots*, trying to live peacefully and with integrity within our families, communities, churches and of course, within our consciences.

The lengths some of us go to in never wanting to put a foot wrong can be quite commendable. Some of us, on the other hand, just want to get by, worrying only about what others see and feeling grateful for our little secrets. But then, if you're like me, this is when your conscience taps you on the shoulder, and you find no peace at all until you've put things right! Such is the dilemma of being brought up as a good little church girl.

Life's journey is such a delicate path of destinations. Detours along the way can make it all so interesting too but oh, the drama and heartache when we lose our way! This applies to all of us in our physical journeys and our spiritual ones. I don't think there's a person on this amazing and often bewildering planet who hasn't, at some point in life, searched for the truth. The way to find this enlightened path can be confusing and troublesome, but our trusty friend *conscience* is always there to help us along.

Gentle Whispers

Of course, there are those in this world who simply don't care whether something is right or wrong! As long as it suits them and their selfish desires, that's all that matters. We all encounter such people in varying degrees, putting us in the predicament of deciding what the right or wrong way is to respond to them. It seems right and wrong will never go away and certainly will never be friends in our active minds!

The irony, though, is that quite often the right and honourable way to act is the hardest. Have you ever told a little white lie to save your own skin or to prevent a hurt or offence to someone else? I have, and paid for it with sleepless nights, a churned-up stomach, and an unsettled conscience until I went to the person and made things right.

This happened not long ago when a dear friend asked to meet another friend and me for lunch. After all the chitter-chatter that happens when three girls get together, there came a lull, and our friend, through tears opened up and apologised for saying things that weren't quite true, just to gain attention. She had heard those *Gentle Whispers* from Heaven convicting her soul that she was not to tell these little fibs anymore because they weren't truthful.

The most beautiful thing, though, was the reason: she realised that God wanted to show her the only attention she truly needed was His. *'Fessing up'* is such a risky thing to do because you know your friends may no longer trust you, or worse, may not want to stay friends. But for us, we were so proud of this dear lady for taking such a huge step in getting back on the right path and trusting us with her confession.

In the end, surely a clear conscience and peace when you say your prayers at night are worth it all. God knows. He understands our weaknesses and frailties, and He's always there speaking to us with loving, convicting whispers to guide us along our way.

"Therefore confess your sins to each other, and pray for each other so that you may be healed., The prayer of a righteous person is powerful and effective." – James 5:16 – NIV

Throughout my life, there have been many times I've lost my way both in the tangible and the spiritual. Thank the Lord for His tender mercies that are always there to bring me back on track. His constant love and patience are something I never take for granted and never tire of sharing with others.

Steadfast Love

The steadfast love of the Lord

Never ceases.

Your mercies never come to an end;

They are new every morning,

new every morning;

Great is your faithfulness, O Lord,

great is your faithfulness.

Edith McNeill, songwriter and composer (1920–2014)

In my work as a pastoral carer, mostly with the elderly, I have seen so many dear souls who are sad and distraught over incidents that happened years ago, times when they made unwise choices and lost their way. Oh, the agony of living with these memories when they could be wiped away in an instant by the grace and forgiveness of their Heavenly Father, who loves them perfectly.

One of the most valued things is when I can take their hand and, through a simple prayer, allow God to gently whisper to their troubled souls that all is well, that they are truly loved, forgiven, and accepted, no matter what their past has been.

Something I've been blessed with over the years is a good memory, or so my family tells me! I certainly don't take this for granted, especially as the years roll by. It's funny how the older memories seem clearer than the more recent ones, but it should all balance out in a few years when the recent ones become the older ones, right? I do hope so! Well, that's my theory anyway.

A story I remember vividly goes back to my primary school days, when I got lost in the great Australian bush. I hope the analogy in this little tale speaks to your heart; it was certainly a huge lesson for me in my younger years.

Gentle Whispers

Girls just want to have fun.

It was one of my friend's birthdays, and six of her closest friends were invited to her home to celebrate. Although the finer details of the party are a little hazy, I still remember the excitement leading up to the day and the events that followed.

The birthday girl had opened her presents, we'd played party games, and eaten far too many sweets and cake. Then her dad had a brilliant idea: why not take the girls for a bushwalk?

The bush track just out of town wasn't far from the first home we'd moved to in that sleepy little town, nestled at the base of a beautiful mountain. I remember my sisters and I playing in those lovely 'nice Australian', lush, green, ferny foothills that backed right onto the boundary of our property.

Oh yes, there's certainly Australian bush that's not lovely at all; scrubby, dry, and dead-looking but I remember this ferny bush as being quite pretty. My parents' words, _"Don't go out of sight of the house,"_ and _"Don't venture past the roadway,"_ are still ringing in my ears.

Maybe it was the exhilaration of six girls high on a sugar fix of lollies, red cordial and cake, or maybe it was my own chance to show off a little to my friends when I suggested that the dad leave us at the start of the bushwalk and pick us up in an hour. I was very convincing, giving information like, "We'll take the main track; it's marked very clearly; I used to live just at the bottom of the mountain; I'd walk up here all the time," hoping it would assure this credulous father that all would be well.

In my defence, though, this was back in the days when children were always out in the open, felt safe playing in the streets, and didn't think for a minute that anything unforeseen or dangerous would take place and it was my Dad's families back yard with our old home, his parents' home, and his brother and sister-in-law's home all within cooee of where we were walking.

The pestering of these adventurous girls was enough to convince this trusting dad, and off we went to explore the wild, promising we'd be at the end of the bushwalk by the designated time, as the birthday girl was wearing her new watch she'd received as a present. After all, it was a council-approved trail, with the estimated walking time written clearly at the start of the track. We had plenty of supplies in our party bags, water in our drink bottles, and honestly, what group of confident girls wanted their father hanging around anyway? Oh dear, so sorry, parents!

With many giggles, songs, skipping, running, jumping, and screaming at the slightest sound in the bush, we made our way along the mountain track. A favourite song back in those days, perfect for such an adventure, was:

I love to go a-wandering along the mountain track,

And as I go, I love to sing,

My knapsack on my back.

Val-deri, val-dera, val-deri, val-dera

ha ha ha ha ha ha

Val-deri, val-dera,

My knapsack on my back.

(The Happy Wanderer,

Words Antonia Ridge,

Music Friedrich W. Moller.

C 1954 Bosworth & Co. Ltd.)

Oh I wonder if you are singing it with me.

We were all having so much fun when, all of a sudden, the track came to an abrupt end! Logs had been placed over the path, showing that this particular walk wasn't yet finished. I felt so silly, had we missed a sign at the beginning saying the track was incomplete, and we should have taken one of the other many walks around this beautiful mountain?

Well, girls being girls, our adventurous thoughts overrode common sense, and off we went to find another track that we were sure couldn't be too far away. I know what you're thinking, Nooooo! Just go back the way you came so you don't get lost! Haha!

As time slipped away, nervousness and fear began to creep into this group of anxious girls, who soon realised they'd made a foolish mistake venturing further into the bush. We certainly hadn't been listening to any sensible *Gentle Whispers* that day, but lessons were learned!

I remember making the decision that it would be best to just stop. Darkness was fast approaching, and it was obvious someone could get seriously hurt if we continued into the deep, dark unknown. From my exploring adventures with my family, I knew there were huge drops over the edges that could lead to a serious accident. As I was explaining this to my friends, the birthday girl burst into tears, followed by another, then another, and another, until we were a group of hysterical, sobbing messes!

Through our tears, we found a safe spot on some rocks, sat down, and made ourselves as comfortable as possible, hoping someone would find us. We shared out the rest of our party treats and drinks as if it were our last meal, then started discussing all the "what ifs" and "buts" about never being found. Oh, it was quite a dramatic scene! Even at our young age, we knew the right thing to do, so why hadn't we done it?

Darkness in the moody, eerie Australian bush can be quite frightening and spooky at the best of times. Imaginations run wild, and every creak or snap of a branch becomes a predator coming to eat you, especially if you were a young girl whose favourite TV show at the time was *Lost in Space* with its weird-looking aliens! (I certainly wasn't a fan, *Lassie* was more my thing!)

It probably wasn't the best time to be telling my friends about Mr Fox, who had come to our little farm at the bottom of the mountain and savagely chomped off the heads of our six beautiful white geese, or about the huge, hungry goanna my mum had shot with Dad's rifle while he was away at army camp!

Poor Marlene, the birthday girl, was so worried about her dad, who by now was probably beside himself with worry, wondering what had happened to us. At times, we would all scream together at the top of our lungs, hoping someone would hear us, then break into song to calm ourselves down. We huddled together, trying to keep warm, when a thought came to me.

Being the good little Sunday school girl of the group, a *Gentle Whisper* came, that we should pray. Yes, even children can hear *Gentle Whispers* and know they're possible. So that's exactly what we did. Childlike prayers are the most precious thing. I've always loved hearing the innocent, simple prayers of my children and now my grandchildren as they've grown up. Through more tears, each girl took her turn pleading with our Heavenly Father to please come and help us in our great time of need, before the boogeyman (who we were all sure camped out on that mountain!) came and took us away, never to be found again.

"God is there, listening for all who pray, for all who pray and mean it." – Psalm 145:18 – The Message

When we'd finished our emotional requests, a calmness seemed to settle over us all. I remember promising God that if we were found safe and sound, I would tell my Sunday school teacher, Mrs Lamont, that prayer really does work!

The six of us sat quietly for a moment, all holding hands, waiting to see how our prayers would be answered. And then, voices. We thought we could hear voices.

"Shhhhhhh," said one of the girls. "Can you hear that?"

There it was again, but this time clearer than before, it was a man's voice calling my name.

"Cathy! Can you hear me? Cathy, where are you? If you can hear me, just yell back, but don't move. I'll come to you."

This hero knew the dangers of rock edges and cliffs on this treacherous mountain. You can imagine the screams of relief and excitement coming from us all! We shouted and yelled, making it quite clear we had heard the voice of the caller who had come to rescue us. What a relief it was, and even more meaningful for me, knowing it was my eldest cousin, Richie, who had become our hero of the moment. I'll never forget his stirring yet comforting words: *"Fancy a Thomas getting lost in her own backyard!"*

It wasn't long before more men, fathers, brothers, uncles, and townsfolk, joined in to help us make the arduous journey down the mountain in the dark, guided by a few torches, back into the arms of worried but relieved parents and family. We were all forgiven too, as there had been no council sign to indicate that the track was incomplete. In the days that followed, quite a *hoo-ha* was made in the local paper and on the television news about the night six excited party girls spent a night on the mountain, all because of a negligent council!

Reflections: Are You Lost? Maybe not literally, but perhaps lost in your thoughts, lost in the circumstances you're living in, unsure of a way out. Maybe you're concerned about a loved one who's lost their way in life and you're worried about their future. Have you ever been the one who's strayed off the safe pathway and found yourself in difficult or dangerous circumstances? Are you now regretting choices you've made and allowing pride, shame, or unbelief to stop you from finding your way back to a better, safer future, a life filled with hope and healing?

Well, if this is you, or someone close to you, let me share a beautiful story from the Bible. I just love this amazing picture of a love so great that nothing can stop us from reclaiming a lost life.

It's found in Luke, where we're told that the Pharisees and religious scholars of the time were criticising Jesus for making friends with sinners, (that would be you and me, because all of us have sinned), and for sharing a meal with them. It goes on to say:

"Suppose one of you had a hundred sheep and lost one. Wouldn't you leave the ninety-nine in the wilderness and go after the lost one until you found it?

When found, you can be sure you would put it across your shoulders, rejoicing, and when you got home, call in your friends and neighbours, saying, 'Celebrate with me! I've found my lost sheep!'

Count on it, there's more joy in heaven over one sinner's (that's you and me again) rescued life than over ninety-nine good people in no need of rescue."

Luke 15:4–7, The Message

Oh, I just love this parable for so many reasons! How amazing would it have been to share a meal with Jesus? To think that He would want to spend time with everyday people, just like you and me, shows what a beautiful and caring man He was. Yes, He was the Son of God, one of the Trinity: Father, Son, and Holy Spirit, but He was also a man who loved people perfectly.

The image of Him noticing that one sheep was missing out of one hundred always amazes me. One hundred is a lot of sheep, yet He noticed that one was gone! He didn't think or say, *"Oh, one won't matter; no one will notice; maybe it'll turn up later."* No! He immediately left the ninety-nine, knowing they'd be safe in their large number, and went looking for the one lost sheep.

How comforting, assuring and secure that makes you feel, especially if you know you're lost, or if you're a parent of a lost child who's gone astray. I find it so encouraging that Jesus didn't stand there saying, *"Stupid sheep, why did you get yourself lost? You silly animal! Do you think I'm just going to wait and see how long it takes you to find your way back?"*

Those weren't His thoughts at all. He left straight away to find the lost sheep.

Maybe your thoughts right now are, *"Well, He sure is taking His time, my child has been lost for years!"* How difficult and heartbreaking that must be, especially if your loved one is living a life you know is harmful to themselves or to others. There are no quick answers here, but what I do know is that there's a perfectly right time when the one you grieve for will be found.

This is where prayer and trust come into the equation. The person you're yearning to see found may not want to be found just yet. Maybe

Gentle Whispers

there are lessons that need to be learned first. Maybe even God is waiting for changes in you before He knows it's the right time.

Be assured, though, Jesus is there. Not judging, often nudging, always loving, and ever protecting lost ones from further harm. Imagine if we had the capacity to see the whole picture, I'm sure we'd be amazed at what God protects us from each day. And you know, He may also be waiting for *you* to stop and listen, just like the little girls lost in the bush.

Jesus IS there

Not judging, often nudging, always loving and ever protecting!

How long has it been since you've gone to your knees with your request before the Lord? Maybe now is the right time to stop and listen for those *Gentle Whispers*. You might just find your way too.

Do you have someone, a son or daughter, father or mother, sister, brother, or friend, who's lost? Then place them in the hands of the Good Shepherd, and trust, pray, and wait expectantly for them to be found. *Shhhhh... can you hear the Gentle Whisper?* He might just be calling your name.

"Don't be afraid, I've redeemed you.

I've called you by name. You're mine.

When you're in over your head,

I'll be there with you.

When you're in rough waters, you will not go down.

When you're between a rock and a hard place,

it won't be a dead end –

because I am God, your personal God,

The Holy of Israel, your Saviour.

I paid a huge price for you…

That's how much you mean to me!

That's how much I love you!

I'd sell off the whole world to get you back,

Trade the creation just for you."

Isaiah 43:1–4, The Message

YES, JUST FOR YOU!

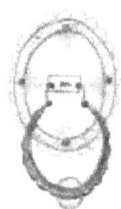

"Never be afraid"

Catherine Grace

Chapter Two
Knock Knock!

Knock, knock, who's there?

Could this be love that's calling?

The door is always open wide.

Knock, knock, who's there?

Now, as the night is falling

Take off your coat and come inside.

John Carter & Geoff Stephens

Recorded by Mary Hopkin – 1970

Are you singing this one too? I remember knowing all the words to this song when I was a teenager living in a small country town. It was one of those towns where it was quite acceptable not to knock on someone's door, but just to call out the person's name, or "coo-ee, is anyone home?" My rather demure Mum was not at all pleased with this country familiarity! Being brought up in the city was quite a different kettle of fish altogether, then she met Herb, a rather rough-and-tumble country boy through and through, so it was the customary country life where they would live for many years. Of course, my beautiful, caring Mum was not a snob; she was just a tad 'proper.' That's not to suggest country people are all 'bumpkins' either! There just seems to be a friendlier, more trusting way about country folk you don't find in the city, or should I say, 'nosier'? Oh dear, am I digging myself into a hole here? I think I'll stop this debate before I end up in real trouble! I will just add, though, that my long-suffering Mum was very gracious to the person who would sit in her car and beep her horn continually, waiting impatiently for someone to go out and see what important errand had brought her a calling on that particular day! It was usually, "Does Herb have any spare eggs?" What a gem she was!

Talking about country and city reminds me of an Aesop fable story my favourite children's author, Beatrix Potter, adapted and called *Johnny*

Gentle Whispers

Townmouse. Johnny loved living in the town, but after meeting another very friendly little mouse, Timmy Willie, from the country, they decided to visit each other and prove once and for all which was best, city or country! I'm sure you all know the moral of this story? Yes, it's to politely disagree and realise there are positives in both. We are all so different, and that's just fine.

I have had the privilege of living in a small country town; a coastal town; another overseas country; two large cities; two country cities; and two coastal cities, in eleven different homes. The most favourite of all these destinations is an older home we renovated in a large country city. When we were transferred to this beautiful four-season city in the country, I felt at home straight away. The colourful autumns of falling leaves, the very chilly winters with sparkly white frosts, and the soft snow were my favourite seasons.

It was in this country town that I really became more familiar with who I was as a person. Getting to know oneself deeply can be very therapeutic. That might sound strange coming from a person who was then in her mid-30s, but it was in these years that my walk with God became deeper and more meaningful. Tragedies, and the ability to fall into some of life's deceitful and harmful traps, make you realise it is a very healthy notion to find out just who you are and why you do the things you do.

Being a child who was brought up in a very strict household with rules that were almost impossible to keep by a very religious 'sergeant-major' father meant I was never allowed to have an opinion. If I did, and my opinion was different from his, I would certainly pay the consequences with a dreadful beating! It was my Dad's way, or no way! I know many of you who are now in your 60s and older would have had the same experiences. The World Wars and living through the Great Depression certainly took their toll on the mental health of some of our parents. I do have to say, though, that in my Dad's later years, it was lovely to see a softening come about from his failing health and seeing his daughters live their lives and bring up their children with more care and understanding than he had. I know his deep faith helped him through many sad reflections in his later years, although sadly, he never said sorry.

One thing I learnt about myself during our time in this beautiful town was that I did not like going and knocking on people's doors anymore! As a child growing up in a smaller country town, my Mum was always sending me on messages to her friends, often with a bunch of violets or a pretty posy from her garden, with a note about the church ladies' group meeting or an invitation to a morning tea. I loved doing this, as I was usually asked in for a glass of cordial and a biscuit. Some of these dear ladies would show me the knitting they were creating or photos of their grandchildren. I felt very safe and quite important, waiting to receive the reply to my Mum's note. This is quite a different scene from our current 'texting,' isn't it?

I think my dislike for knocking on doors came from all the different moves we had over the years with my husband's work. In the beginning, setting up house in unfamiliar cities without knowing who the neighbours were would see me knocking on their doors to introduce ourselves and hopefully have friendly relationships. Waiting for neighbours to come and knock on our door often didn't happen, hence my previous comment about cities being a little unfriendly. As the moves progressed, to be quite honest, it all became too bothersome, plus the fact I may be disturbing something important, after all, who wants to be a nuisance on someone's busy day? Not me! So in the end, it was our ninth move and a bad experience that sadly saw the knocking stopped. The making of friends was usually done through playgroups and churches, which worked well, as no knocking on doors was required.

As my own children were growing up, like myself, they were sometimes sent on an errand to a neighbour's house, but only if I knew it was a safe house, of course, and this usually took some bribing with extra pocket money or a treat! Now I know, on a scale of world events, this is all quite trivial, but it does set the scene for our next story. When a Gentle Whisper nudges you to go and knock on the door of an unknown neighbour across the road, what is one to do?

Gentle Whispers

Dear little Lily

It was time to take Betsy, our little Pomeranian poodle, for her walk. Hubby was miles away travelling for work; the children were all at school, and now it was time for some fresh air before the rush of washing, ironing, cleaning, endless errands, art studio lessons etc. all in the short hours before it was the end of school time.

One of the things I loved to do most was take our little dog for a walk through a nearby park, where a creek flowed, ducks swam, and birds sang. In spring, bright yellow daffodils danced in the wind beneath the birch trees, and in autumn, colourful leaves fluttered to the ground, creating a beautiful carpet of joy for all the children who loved to run and jump into it, hoping for a crunchy landing. Just next to this area of the park was a grand Cape Cod cottage, which I was sure would one day be our home. Dream as I might, the next move came along, and all my whimsical thinking became history!

I remember this particular day very well. On our way home, I started having thoughts about knocking on the door of a home across the road from us. It was a beautiful corner home we had admired since living there, that faced an adjacent street to ours. At first, I put these little whispers off as being inquisitiveness. I had seen the lady of the manor a couple of times and waved; she would politely wave back. By the time I arrived home, I had completely talked myself out of going and knocking at her door, as I really didn't know why I would be calling. What would I say? Would she be home? Was I being intrusive, or would I look like a busybody? My excuses went on and on.

As I turned to walk up our driveway, the whisper turned into the thought: if I walked past her house, the lady might be sitting on her front verandah. Giving Betsy a little tug, we started to walk around the corner, then right past the house, and then around the block, as no one was on the verandah! Well, at least walking around the block gave me time to think up what I would say to this unsuspecting neighbour. I know! I could ask her to join my art classes in my studio, which was next to my home. That's it God, isn't it? She is lonely and could join my classes!

Catherine Grace

So off Betsy and I went again, this time ascending the stairs of the rather grand two-story home and knocking on the front door. We waited, then knocked again, and again, and again. Oh, seriously! What has this all been about? Obviously, no one was home. I was about to turn away, feeling rather silly and thinking I must have heard the whisper wrong, when the door opened slowly, revealing a very sad-looking, pale-faced tiny lady who would not have been even five feet tall. Her blonde hair was tousled, and my first thought was that I had disturbed her sleep.

"Can I help you?" she asked quietly. I explained I was Cathy from across the road, and before I could say any more, she interrupted me rather firmly.

"Why have you come? Why would you knock on my door right now?" Her words trailed off, and then she beckoned me inside. I looked down at Betsy, but she was invited in as well, with the explanation that the lady loved little dogs and had admired Betsy many times through her window.

After exchanging names and small talk, Lily shared her very sad story. At the very moment I had knocked on her door, Lily had been upstairs with a bottle of sleeping pills in her hand, ready to end it all. The struggle with lupus had become too much, and her overbearing, narcissistic husband had become too difficult and abusive to live with. Alcohol was no longer dulling the pain, and for this deeply disturbed little lady, sleeping pills were the only way she could escape.

You can imagine my shock, and then my relief, that I *had* knocked on this dear lady's door. I explained to her the struggle I had with actually responding to the Gentle Whisper I had thought of during my walk. I also suggested contacting a beautiful couple in our church, who were retired pastors and could help her. This couple had beautiful hearts and were trained in pastoral care and counselling more than I was. They worked with people in the community who just couldn't cope with life any more.

Phone calls were made, appointments arranged, and the assurance that Lily could knock on my door any time seemed to help her. I was still reluctant to leave, knowing the predicament she had been in before I knocked. It was a perfect time for all of this to take place, as her husband was not home, but what to do? Those pills were still upstairs! Taking a deep breath, I asked if I could stay with her until her husband came home, but in the meantime, could we please tip the tablets down the toilet? Knowing what I know now about the environment and how to do things correctly in the disposing of medicines, this was probably not very environmentally friendly, but this lady's life was at stake. She agreed wholeheartedly, knowing there was hope and realising there was a God in Heaven who cared enough to send a stranger to knock on her door that day.

There is a most remarkable end to this story. Lily received all the help she so desperately needed. With counselling, her marriage was healed, and her husband became more tolerant and compassionate to his wife's needs. Years of watching her health decline and not being able to fix it had caused severe frustration and behaviour he ended up being very sorry for. He became good friends with our retired church couple, and they even started attending their church again, which they hadn't set foot in for many years.

Another wonderful surprise for both Lily and me was that she had a beautiful hidden talent in art. She was very excited to join my classes and painted alongside the other artists who came each Tuesday for seven years, until it became too difficult for her to manoeuvre the brush. It was such a joy to see her laughing, painting, and singing along to the music I played as we painted. Her sweet voice was classically trained, and she had sung for many years in choirs and choral groups. What a blessing this dear friend was to us.

Meeting her two grandchildren, who came in the years after her life-saving day, was also such a privilege. The joy and happiness were so evident whenever she spoke of them, and this has been a constant reminder to me to never take Gentle Whispers lightly. God always knows, has a plan, and loves to lavish His children with the most amazing surprises! Not only was Lily's life saved that day, but a beautiful friendship was also given to me.

A truly tender and marvellous wonder to witness in the months to follow was seeing Lily grow so close to God. Jesus became her best friend, helping her through many struggles during her days and those ohhh-so-painful nights. Her spirit soared like a bird in flight when she spoke of Him. She would share how comforting Gentle Whispers had become a part of her days too, even in what she would paint and to whom she would give her masterpieces. I am overwhelmed by the goodness of God!

This does raise the question, though: why didn't God just heal her? Well, I'm afraid I must leave that question to a more mature theologian and trust God, who knows best in *all* things. He sees the bigger picture and where each piece of the puzzle fits. As I have had my own health struggles over the years, this question often lingers on the tip of my tongue when frustrations get the better of me. In the end, though, when I give these questions to God, peace comes, and more often than not, I can see the wisdom and the good that arise from leaving it all in His capable hands. One thing I am sure of is that God will never leave or abandon us. His presence and enabling will help us through any situation we face on even the most challenging day.

Reflections: It is actually quite remarkable but not surprising to note since this day, I don't seem to have the same dislike for knocking on people's doors. For whatever reason that may be, I find it easier now, and I am reassured that fear is there not to hinder us or bring anxiety, but to make us stronger and help us become an overcomer.

> *"For God will never give you the spirit of fear,*
> *but the Holy Spirit will give you*
> *mighty power, LOVE and self-control."*
> 2 Timothy 1:7

Ohhh, there it is the glorious word, *LOVE*! God's surprises are a token of His amazing love for us. I have never met a parent yet who doesn't love to give beautiful gifts to their children. If, like me, we search high and low to buy the perfect gift, there is a promise in the Word that our Heavenly Father is not going to give us a snake if He knows we desire a fish. He knows us all so deeply and knows just what will bring us joy, healing, a bounce in our step, and warm fuzzies to bless our hearts. He also knows what we need to overcome in our lives to make us stronger, bolder, and able to be used more by His mighty hand in this world we call home. Never underestimate the help and even life you can bring to a person by following one little Gentle Whisper. It can bring so much joy and peace into their souls, just knowing you cared enough to share with them and to be an instrument of God's perfect love.

Peaceful Sounds

Sounds of rippling water on the lake's edge;
a distant whipbird song from a nearby hedge.

Sounds of silence, of solitude and peace…
I've waited so long to have this release.

So I let go of stresses, the noises that harm,
and breathe in the comfort of stillness and calm.

We've made it this far so we can go on,
stronger and wiser because of the one…

…who has brought us this far in His perfect Love.
C. G. 2022

I truly am so humbled to know that in desiring to be an overcomer in an area I was struggling with, God not only did a work in me, but He also saved someone's life with the latter being the most amazing work of His love. To be used by God is the most awesome honour anyone can be given.

Catherine Grace

Maybe you are struggling with something at this very moment. I wonder if God is there with Gentle Whispers for you to be the overcomer He wants you to be. He so desperately wants you to be free in every area of your life. That is why He gave us Jesus. Won't you turn an ear to Him today? Won't you be brave and open your heart to Him today, and listen ever so intently for the whispers I am sure are coming your way? It's really quite easy, you know. All you need to say is: *"Jesus, I need you."*

"Never be afraid to trust an unknown future,

To a known God."

Cornelia Arnolda Johanna "Corrie" ten Boom

April 1892 – April 1983

Gentle Whispers

Chapter Three: "I'm Sure You Can!"

"I think I can,

I think I can,

I think I can,

I know I can."

Watty Piper— author

The Little Engine That Could

Platt & Munk Publishers, 1930

An inferiority complex really is… well, a very complex state of affairs! Today, it has many different diagnosed names, including Oedipal complex, Electra complex, or Oedipus complex. You, like me, probably know it as low self-esteem.

Now, I'm sure a very clever psychologist out there, with a string of letters after his or her name, would tell me there's a huge difference between an inferiority complex and low self-esteem, but for the sake of not confusing the issue too much, maybe Mr Google's definition will help:

"An inferiority complex is characterised

by constant feelings of inadequacy or

insecurity in your daily life due to

a belief that you are physically

or mentally inferior to others."

(According to the American Psychological Association.)

Do you know this debilitating feeling? "I think I can, I think I can", but more often than not, really believing it's "I know I can't"!

Maybe it isn't even an inferiority complex or low self-esteem either, but now I'm confusing you, aren't I? Well, I'll put it this way: if you lack confidence, have negative feelings about yourself, feel unloved, awkward in the company of others, incompetent, and fall easily into the trap of criticising yourself, then you're probably suffering from a very common dose of some form of low self-worth.

There are many causes for having this problem, ranging from an unhappy childhood where parents or teachers were extremely critical; poor academic performance in school or sport; bullying from classmates or work colleagues; not being accepted because of your colour, race, or social standing; to stressful relationships such as marriage breakdowns and financial difficulties.

As I've hinted before, if you're the same or a similar age to me, then a good old belting from a domineering, controlling parent, or the cane from a teacher who didn't know better, was probably part of everyday life.

I don't remember how old I was when I received my first belting or beating. I was very young, and I know it was before school years. The reason for receiving such discipline was always rather minor, but *spare the rod and spoil the child* was definitely how it was in the good old days.

Ohhh, the stories many of us *could* tell you! But for the sake of *"honour your father and mother,"* as the Good Book instructs us to do, and in acknowledging the goodness Dad did have in his very damaged mind and soul, from his own childhood and those dreadful war years, it's probably best if I just flutter over those memories like a sparrow in flight.

I'll never understand why the armed forces didn't have counselling or psychological help for war neurosis victims put in place for when these soldiers came home. They were actually instructed to put on a stiff upper lip and not tell a soul of the traumas and devastation they'd seen and been a part of when they were forced into battle.

I wrote these words a few years ago when I was deliberating such thoughts:

> *To all our brave war veterans, past and present...*

Catherine Grace

<u>We will remember.</u>
When Anzac Day is over,
the wreaths all sadly fade,
all that's left to ponder is
the heartbreak war has made.

It's nice to be remembered,
'Lest we forget' the pain,
but secrecy reminds us
there is nothing left to gain.

Brave heroes, tell your stories.
Break the silence, code, and shame.
Don't carry guilt or torment,
no, there isn't any blame.

We need to know the sacrifice,
for how else will we learn?
You all deserve a peaceful life,
as war must not return!

We understand the stories
are just too sad to bear,
but surely, as we listen,
the load we too can share.

Gentle Whispers

You gave your lives to save us,
a gift we can't repay...
A soothing balm of friendship
may help you through the day.

Is it too late, dear soldier?
So many of you gone...
But we will still remember –
we'll tell your stories, sing your songs.

Tell the truth about the journey!
Yes, hold those heads up high.
It's the only way for healing,
to let your spirits fly.

C.G. – Anzac Day 2020

It wasn't until 1980, when a study took place at Monash University by a team led by Professor Christina Twomey, that war neurosis, now known as Post-Traumatic Stress Disorder, was officially recognised. Up until then, it was actually documented, *quote*, "These soldiers carry some inherent frailty or mental weakness, some predisposition!"

This makes me so upset and devastated for these brave soldiers, one of whom was my dad! Most of these soldiers were just boys, seeing and having to take part in the intensities of battle, far beyond their qualifications or knowledge of what extreme violence, destruction, and bloody mortality lay ahead of them. We can only hope they were able to hear the Gentle Whispers from above, as God promises never to leave us or forsake us, especially in our times of deep need.

Now, where was I after that little detour? Oh yes, the first caning I received at school was when I was six years old, in first class, from Miss

Lane! Yes, Miss Lane certainly could swing the cane! To this day, I can identify the feelings of embarrassment and fear, made worse by this cruel act taking place in front of the whole class! The absolute unfairness of the scenario was that I was the innocent party, and the guilty person was the boy sitting next to me, and I even remember his name, ha! Taking the cane seemed a better option, though, than the terror of having to face Reggie in the playground at recess!

So, for whatever reason you have been, or are, down on yourself, if it isn't dealt with or help isn't sought, it can lead to harmful results. If this is you, I hope you seek counsel and grow in knowing how uniquely beautiful you really are. You can take this as a direct Gentle Whisper to your heart.

"When you believe that you are beautiful,

other people are bound to think the same."

Anon.

Needless to say, an unhealthy self-worth is something I battled with from a very early age. I really don't mind telling you this, because if my journey can be of some help to someone else, it's worth it. I'd rather my life be an open book read in the light than an old, stained, ragged book sitting on a dark shelf collecting dust, or, as the Good Book says, hiding it under a bushel. The latter is of no use to anyone really, and such a waste.

One of my beliefs in life is that we all have a story to tell, and if we are brave enough, it is those stories that can lift someone else up, help dust them off, and encourage them on their way. It is also very helpful to hear stories of victory, as we gain healing and can put those negative traits behind us. As the years have journeyed on, I am so grateful I am not the person I used to be, all glory to God, who loves me so very much and only wants the very best for me!

Over the years, I have appreciated the true stories I've read where people share their life lessons, their struggles of ups and downs, and even their mistakes, with the hope that it will shed light on a situation other may be experiencing at that very moment.

Now, let's get to the point of this prelude to the next extraordinary story of the Gentle Whisper, which really did blow me away with its answer to a heart that had been yearning for years to find out just what was the point of 'me'? If it sounds familiar, you may have read part of it in my first book *Beauty All Around*, but please stay tuned, as this is the full story (she says with a wink)!

Everything IS Possible…

Like many women of my era, I found myself privileged to be a stay-at-home mother of three beautiful children, and yes, it was a privilege. Being a mum was something I absolutely loved. Each day was an adventure that had been planned the night before as I lay awake, waiting for Mr Sandman to come.

With a daddy who had to travel for work and be away from his family, we decided very early on that our children would not suffer or miss out because of their dad's days away, working to make our ends meet. Looking back on it now, the years have just flown by, as I now watch so many parents juggle their own lives, being the remarkable gifts they are to this world we live in, and also to their own families and children.

Some mums stay at home for a couple of years. Some dads stay at home too. My own once-ancient opinion that 'mums must stay at home' has slowly softened and changed as I've seen how they all have such capacity to manage, to be both working parents and homemakers. I might add, though, that in my day it was just not acceptable. Good grief, I can imagine the uproar if I had put my children in childcare, especially with my hubby being a travelling dad!

So, when all our children were at school and I had some spare hours in my day, I decided it was time to see what else I could bring to the table, for my own life, my family's lives, and others. So, I started art classes. There was a beautiful walk through a park near our home that led me to a pretty picture-book cottage covered in Boston ivy.

I would take our little dog for a walk through this park most days, which was complete with a babbling brook, better known in Aussie terms as a running creek, where ducks of every description would play away the hours with their ducking and diving.

Catherine Grace

This particular day, I decided to venture a little further, where a most welcome God surprise was waiting for me. A sign on the front door of this quaint cottage beckoned me inside with the invitation of decorative art classes. I do apologise again if you've read some of this story in my first book, but stay tuned, it does have another life lesson! God does love not wasting one moment of our daily lives, don't you think?

Well, I certainly did take to this art form like those ducks taking to water, and after months of learning and practising, my teacher started encouraging me to do a course so I could teach others this historical European art form.

So, you know what happened, don't you? Low self-worth came banging on my door, not as a polite knock, but as a defiant *"you could never do that"* in full force! The thought was supposed to have been pushed way back in the cobwebs of my mind, never to resurrect again, or so I thought.

Over the following months, I worked very hard painting orders for people and even put some of my works into a craft shop near where I lived. This did take a measure of esteem to be able to achieve, but for me, it was easier to think someone would buy my art than it was to imagine myself standing out the front and teaching it.

Do you remember all those career advising courses and interviews we had at school? Mine always came back saying I was most suited to the creative area, so I had my heart set on something to do with art.

Maybe it was the first-prize award I'd received for my *carnation in a vase* painting, which my teacher at school had entered into a local competition. Or maybe it was the cute little Holly Hobbie-style drawings of girls with ponytails, ribbons, and big eyes I was always doodling away at.

So you can imagine my excitement when our local technical college was advertising for a ticket writing and window dressing course at the end of my last year of school. I ran all the way home to tell my parents after seeing the sign in the college window, but was greeted with a very firm, "NO! You will be going to secretarial school, and you will get a real job!"

Gentle Whispers

This course was in the town half an hour away from our home, with the added stipulation: "If it was good enough for your sister, it is good enough for you!" So that's exactly what I did. I'd learnt many years before that there was no point in arguing, or there would be consequences!

The days turned into months while I was home alone for many hours, with hubby away and our children at school. It was just myself, our dog, chooks, ducks, bunnies, my paintbrush, and the morning tea catch-ups with 'like-situated friends' who were finding it hard to re-enter the workforce after being at home raising children for so long!

One saving grace was that our phone would sometimes ring for some part-time work at the Electoral Commission during school hours at election time, which did help financially, especially when recounts would go on for months, but the feelings of worthlessness were slowly creeping back in like a misty fog on a damp winter's evening. I know these feelings often hit women of this age when their nest is becoming less nestled as their children go out into the big, wide, wonderful world. Gosh, I had a studio of women sharing these stories for many years.

I continued to paint and paint, even venturing more into the mainstream forms of art. Quaint cottages and scenes were starting to overtake the decorative floral and folk art designs, but the paintings that always sold the quickest were the traditional European historical art pieces I would paint on boxes, trays, signs, well, anything really. My hubby used to say, "Better not leave that sitting there or Cathy will paint it!"

Then a Gentle Whisper I will never forget came knocking on my door. It was a sweet little lady who had bought one of my art pieces at the craft shop where I sold my creations. This dear lady, with short white curly hair, dressed in a pale pink twinset and beige slacks, was exactly that, quite sweet and little! Fay really was tiny, and her soft voice was even fainter.

If you're still back at the twinset words and don't, for the life of you, know what it is, well, back in *the old days* twinsets were all the fashion. *Twin*, because they were nearly exactly the same, and a *set*, because it was a short-sleeved knitted top with a matching long-sleeved knitted cardigan you wore over the top. The reason being, you could easily take off the cardigan if you were too hot. They really were the height of fashion, with all the leading lady film stars owning one of every colour, complete with pearl buttons down the cardigan front, giving the impression you were quite well off!

I leaned in to hear what this rather nervous little lady was saying, her words being as dainty as she was. "Hello, my name is Fay and I live not far from here. I bought one of your beautiful boxes from the craft shop and I just love the artwork so much. One of the sales ladies gave me your address, I hope you don't mind, because I'm wondering, do you happen to teach? Do you do art classes?"

You can imagine my shock! I invited her in and showed her all the pieces I was still working on. My art table was just off the lounge room in an area we weren't really sure what it was there for, except to fit a table to do something on. Maybe it had been an office area for the previous owners. It had a half wall between it and the dining room, with a lovely view over the front garden. It was a peaceful place where I could while away the hours perfectly as I created my pieces to sell.

We chatted away for quite a while, with the word *teach* still floating around in the back of my mind. I wondered if she had been a fly on the wall when my art teacher had suggested teaching to me many months before, or if it was my own thoughts and a quick prayer about the same, but I'd just fobbed them off, thinking, *I could never do that!*

But there it was, the Gentle Whisper had floated in on angel wings from a sweet little lady who was brave enough to knock on my door, something I would eventually be brave enough to do. Remember the struggles I had with Lily?

I promised Fay I would look into teaching, but if I did, I'd want to do it properly, so I would seek out an accredited course. If she didn't mind, though, I could always practise on her while I studied. She jumped at the idea, and we painted together for the whole two years while I studied the course by distance education.

During this time, I was privileged to have tutors who were university and senior high school art teachers who went above and beyond to help the many students like me who were seeking a career in art but didn't want to take years and years of extra study to get there. Many of us did not have our Higher School Certificate and had left school with the Year 10 School Certificate to get a job or do further study at Technical College, like I had done. This fact, in itself, left one feeling of lesser worth, especially when some of your friends had continued on and took great pleasure in letting you know it!

How grateful I was that this Teacher's Accreditation course was available, and what a blessing Fay was, encouraging me with her feedback and support. It wasn't long until this friend had spread the word and other ladies were coming along to my classes too.

After I had completed the accredited course and had my certificate framed, my family decided it was time Mum had her own studio. The dining table just wasn't big enough anymore. This did come with mixed feelings, though, as it meant our eldest son was leaving home to start his own adventures, but his room would be perfect. It was easily converted to a beautiful council-approved studio on the side of the house that was easily accessible from the street.

In the first studio, named *Garden Gallery*, I held three classes a day with six to eight ladies in each class. It was such a privilege to take these precious ladies (and only one very brave gentleman in all those years) on their own journeys of self-discovery and the knowledge that they actually did have gifts they never thought possible. How blessed was I to be part of their lives during this time!

To be able to build a little self-worth, self-acceptance, and self-love into these dear ladies' lives with a splash of paint and a paintbrush is something I am so grateful for!

Since then, there have been two other studios in another two homes, yes, another work move and then a downsize, and another name change (someone stole my registered *Garden Gallery* name, and I couldn't be bothered fighting them for it!). So *Garden Terrace Studio* it was. And now, after 22 years of teaching, and no longer holding structured classes but an art friendship group instead (the old girl is slowing down, and retirement adventures are in the wings), I am just so glad I took notice of the Gentle Whisper that touched my ears so softly that day.

I await the next Gentle Whisper, which I'm sure will show me the road ahead. How exciting, God surprises are always worth waiting for!

Oh, and back to the name *Garden Terrace Studio*. When I was looking for a new name, it became quite a family affair. All sorts of names were being thrown around, but none of them really fitted. It wasn't until our eldest son arrived home with his beautiful wife from teaching in England that all became clear.

He was standing on the side verandah where the space was being renovated into the second council-approved studio. The garden was directly out the front of this studio and was all terraced, with a beautiful big rock wall leading down the face of the hill in terraces, to a path that finished at the stairs of the studio.

Straight away, as if by a Gentle Whisper (I'm sure it was), he said, "Garden Terrace Studio." Oh, it was perfect! We quickly checked, and the name wasn't being used, so I grabbed it straight away.

About a month later, my mum, who had been searching our family tree for years, rang me all excited! She had just received new information to say her grandfather from Hartlepool Headland had lived in *Garden Terrace*!

So, you do know this is not a coincidence, don't you?

Reflections: I'm sure you know that everyone has to take full responsibility for their own feelings of inferiority. Yes, I definitely had reasons for these feelings, but everyone has the ability to improve themselves and to overcome. Blame will only take you down the drain! There are so many self-help courses, counselling opportunities, books, groups, etc. available today. For me, the best course was Christian Prayer Counselling and opening up my heart to the One I believed loved me the most, yes, my Heavenly Father.

I'm reminded of a quote I came across not long ago from a very wise lady who posted it on Instagram:

Gentle Whispers

"No one can make you feel inferior without your consent."

Eleanor Roosevelt, 1884–1962

Just imagine the wonderful opportunities that may be waiting for you, just like they were for me. I could have revelled in excuses like *but I don't even have a university degree!* I could have taken seriously the words of a very uncaring person who told me when I first started my studio, "That's not real art!" Well, in her oil-painting landscape eyes, maybe acrylic decorative art wasn't. I will say, though, her paintings were absolutely beautiful, but definitely more impressionistic and not decorative art at all.

It has been a controversial topic that never seems to have a clear answer, but in my studies over the years, Fine Art is often celebrated for its individualism, originality, and personal expression, while Decorative Art in all its forms, which includes European Folk Art such as German *Bauernmalerei*, the Netherlands' *Hindeloopen*, and Norway's *Rosemaling*, to name a few, is deeply rooted in tradition and cultural context. Decorative Art is often passed down through generations, with each generation adding its unique touches to the art form. This art form is predominantly functional or utilitarian visual art created by hand, with its aim being to prolong the survival of tradition.

One of my art tutors over the years has just received her doctorate, which included her bachelor's, two master's, and then her doctorate. I take my hat off to her and admire her determination and ability! Maybe I could have chosen the same road when she invited me to, but for me, it was important to follow the Gentle Whisper and teach, rather than have my head in a book for all those years.

We all have different paths to take, and each path leads to a wonderful destination, doing what we believe we are called to do. For me, it was sharing the beauty of creation and history through art, and building beauty and confidence into each person who came to my classes and would say, "Oh, I could never paint that!" Ohhh yes, you can!

Catherine Grace

It also led me to writing, a gift I never thought would become a book (and now a second one), along with three short stories and poetry that have been published to date. This may not seem very significant to many people. I know I will never be a world changer, but I am changing the world for those who have given me the privilege of helping them in their creative journey. This fills me with so much joy and peace.

My Heavenly Father always had a plan and purpose for my life, even when I didn't know it, and was ever so patient with His Gentle Whispers until I *got it*! So, I'll say it again, if He did it for me, He will most certainly do it for you too!

I do hope my little story helps those of you who aren't sure where your road ahead is leading, or who are wondering, *what is the point of you?* Maybe the winding garden path that looks like a dead end is where you are right now? Well, can I encourage you to look a little closer at what is just ahead? Maybe it's a detour, oh look, it's only a couple more steps! Yes, you can do it! You are being cheered on, and Heaven is watching with those Gentle Whispers that are just waiting to touch your sweet little ears!

> *"For every failure, there is an*
>
> *alternative course of action.*
>
> *You just have to find it.*
>
> *When you come to a roadblock,*
>
> *take a detour."*
>
> *Mary Kay Ash— 1918–2001*

Have you ever thought that your detour may be to share your own stories? I never thought I would want people to know all my hidden secrets! I still don't, really, but through following the detours and listening to the Gentle Whispers, here I am, sharing my simple life stories again. Ones I only ever thought were important to me, and then, in the middle of one of those life lessons, I came across this enlightening quote:

Gentle Whispers

"Each experience we have had —
regardless of how embarrassing, sad,
shameful or even seemingly insignificant —
has the potential to be used redemptively
by God
in the people whose paths cross ours.
Give your stories away and get ready
for God
to use them beyond your wildest
hopes and dreams."
By Christine Wood

Yes, give them away! Take the risk and be brave. I do hope you too will share your stories. You have so much to give to your world! Your life experiences are so important, and you just never know how God will use them, even beyond your wildest hopes and dreams!

...with His perfect Love

Chapter Four:
Love Is A Many Splendid Thing

"My Dad's favourite score of music"

From the movie Love is a Many-Splendored Thing

Music score – Sammy Fain

Composer/conductor – Alfred Newman

(Lyrics – Paul Francis Webster)

I don't think it is a coincidence at all that this music score, which my Dad said was his favourite arrangement of music ever, was written in 1955, the year of my birth. It also won the Academy Award in 1956 for Best Original Song and mentions my birth month too.

Love is a many splendored thing.

It's the April rose that only grows in the early spring.

Love is nature's way of giving a reason to be living,

the golden crown that makes a man a king.

When I first found this out, it really did touch my heart. Like many fathers from the 'good old days' or men who served in the war, my Dad found love one of the hardest emotions to show, except to his dear wife, thank goodness. Moments of tenderness between them were always a blessing to witness while growing up, so knowing I was born out of a loving relationship has always been special to me.

One thing he was, though, was very gifted, informative, and educated in music. He had a natural talent for singing tenor, playing brass instruments, and writing music. During his life, he played in many bands, leading bands in the Salvation Army, the Royal Australian Engineers band, the Army cadet school bands, and also led choirs. His ability to harmonise and teach others to sing in parts was always appreciated by those who had the privilege of singing and listening. It has been a joy to me, seeing some of these gifts being passed on over the years to the generations that followed.

Gentle Whispers

The actual score of this song is documented as being "one of the most romantic and beautiful scores ever written. Newman's stunning variations on the Fain and Webster song, along with his own gorgeous secondary themes, create a unique atmosphere with a swirling tenderness that's almost indescribable," said recording studio Kritzerland. I hope you have the opportunity to listen to this brilliant and moving piece of music. It is still available and often played on the radio and YouTube. The words to this moving music are very touching too, as was the movie, but it was the music score that Dad always spoke of. I actually never heard him mention the storyline or lyrics, they are lovely, though.

So why is *Love a Many-Splendored Thing*? Splendour in the Oxford Dictionary explains: **splendid** – a. magnificent, admirable, glorious, excellent; **splendour** – n. great brightness, magnificence, to shine. Oh yes, I would have to totally agree. Maybe you are someone who finds it difficult to accept love because of past hurts or circumstances, but when something splendid does touch your heart, it really is healing and a wonderful experience.

It can be the beauty of the lushest rose with perfume so sweet; the touch of a loved one's hand on your cheek, letting you know all will be well. The excitement a dog shows you when you walk through the door certainly does exude all glorious feelings of love for both dog and owner. Nature has always been one way I feel love. Over the years, I have found it so easy to feel I am loved while looking at the most magnificent mountain or valley view, especially if the mountain is being hugged by mist and fog, and the valley is as green as Kermit the Frog. Rugged ocean coastlines always excite me, where the waves crash magnificently against the rugged rocky cliffs; pretty flowers where each petal is so delicate and unique; and ducks bobbing up and down at the lake without a care in the world. All of these experiences bring feelings of love to my whole being.

Are you wondering why? Well, I'll tell you, it's because it is about the only perfect love in all of creation. Here it is in a hymn I have known and sung since I was a little girl:

All things bright and beautiful,

Catherine Grace

All creatures great and small,

All things wise and wonderful,

The Lord God made them all.

Cecil F. Alexander, pub. 1848

The timeless hymn goes on to list nearly everything in creation: flowers; little birds singing; purple-headed mountains; rivers running; sunrises at the break of day and sunsets at dusk that brighten up the sky; cold winds in winter; summer sun; ripe fruits; tall trees; meadows where we play; rushes by the water. Dear Cecil obviously had a deep love for her Heavenly Father.

It is written in the Good Book that after God had made everything, He saw it all and saw it was very good. Very good? There is our first lesson in humility recorded in Genesis right there. How about magnificent, wonderful, even splendid! Actually, I don't think there is an adjective in the whole dictionary that would come close to being able to describe the beauty of God and nature. For me, the beauty of nature has been my safe place. Knowing God made all this for me to enjoy shows His great love for me, and His love is perfect in every way.

My faith is certainly built on God's love for me, so I must include here, when talking about love, the greatest of all love found in John 3:16:

For here is the way God loved the world –

He gave His only, unique Son as a gift.

So now everyone who believes in Him

will never perish but experience

everlasting life.

The Passion Translation

I grew up knowing this verse in the older King James translation:

For God so loved the world, that He gave His only begotten Son, that whosoever believeth in Him, should not perish but have everlasting life.

Doesn't the more modern translation above bring it to life? Love is mentioned in the Bible 714 times. It is said nothing is greater than love, not even faith and hope. Love is defined as patient; kind; it does not envy or boast; it is not arrogant or rude. It isn't selfish; it is not irritable or resentful; it does not rejoice at wrongdoing, but rejoices with the truth. We are instructed to love God with all our heart, soul, strength, and mind. And we are to love our neighbour as we love ourselves. The Bible also says the greatest of all these things is LOVE, and there is no greater love than to lay down one's life for one's friends.

Is it no wonder the thing most under threat in the world today is LOVE? I do not want to be preachy here, so I have listed these thoughts in paraphrase. Be assured, though, Satan, the founder of the opposite of love, is the one who is having his way with hate and selfishness in the world. He is the one making so much havoc with suicide, self-hate, and the lack of love, and why hostility is at an all-time high. As you know, I am no great theologian, but I do have a heart for God and His truth, so please forgive me if you think I have lost the plot in my thinking of the hereafter in the following story!

Goodness, the last thing I want to do is give false information, so I will leave you to ponder these matters for yourself! I want to lead into my next story on this subject of love with you knowing *Gentle Whispers* can come along at the most unexpected times for the most healing of purposes. I have written of the beautiful hymn in previous writings, but for some intentional, God-knowing reason, here it is again, when love was put back in its rightful place, the very centre of my heart.

With Sympathy

(Just advising for those who may benefit

from knowing – this story contains content

of the passing of my Dad)

The thought of it being a rather quiet, uneventful weekend was short-lived. My husband and eldest son of our household were at a men's conference in Sydney, where hundreds of men from all over the country had gathered for a weekend of teaching and mateship. These conferences were a real blessing to the men who gathered every year. The women of this denomination had already had their women's conference earlier in the year, and now it was the men's turn. So it was my other two children and I who were left to live it up a little, with lunch out and an afternoon of movies. Does anyone know someone who has watched *While You Were Sleeping* six times? I do!

It wasn't long into the first movie when we were rudely interrupted by the telephone. Ohhh bother! The caller on the other end of the line sounded rather shaken, and it took me a couple of times to gather what was being said and by whom! Then, like a dark cloud of heaviness, reality struck with a thud, my Dad had been taken to hospital by ambulance, suffering from a heart attack. Yes, another heart attack. This wasn't an isolated event with my Dad, but after suffering many, along with numerous heart-related surgeries including bypasses, pacemaker and defibrillator devices over 25 years, we all knew there wasn't much else that could be done for Dad's very damaged and troubled heart.

Our daughter, who is very good at organising, especially in emergency situations, managed to have my bags packed and her rather stunned Mum choofed off into the car, on the way to a little country town one and a half hours' drive away where Dad had been taken to hospital. The phone call seemed to convey an urgency to get there as quickly as possible, so my first thought was that Dad must have still been with us. It was a blessing not to have to worry about leaving the children at home, as our daughter was of an age to be able to care for her little brother. I also instructed her to try and get onto her Dad at the conference, who was there with another of her grandfather's sons-in-law.

As I was driving, my thoughts were racing. One thing on my mind was a request I had been praying about for quite a few years – I really wanted to hear my Dad say he loved me. I didn't think this was a huge request at all, but as the years rolled by and the words were never spoken, I did spend many a moment wondering why. At times, I had told my Dad I loved him, but the words were either ignored or shrugged off with a "humph" or "none of that now!" In the end, I just gave up, but I must say it was lovely seeing Dad mellow in his latter years. He did find it easier to show our children kindness, and his visits were always enjoyed by listening to his funny jokes and stories. He loved shouting us tea, with his cheeky saying being "I'm cooking tonight!" Chinese was his favourite, and he also loved helping out in many generous ways when things were needed.

I remember once Mum and Dad visited when our rather overused clothes dryer had decided it had experienced quite enough of these rainy, cold winter days and was refusing to work. Washing was strung all around the house, and Dad's voice boomed, "So now you are living in a Chinese laundry, are you?" It wasn't until they had left that I found a cheque, written out for cash and signed by him, lying on the dining room table. I guessed it was to buy a new clothes dryer. After enquiring, well yes, of course it was, but no mushy thank you would be tolerated at all! These subtle ways of showing love were always appreciated, and I wondered if it was his way of trying to make up for all the abuse of my younger years, but I did still yearn to hear the words **I LOVE YOU**.

I normally enjoyed the country drive between our home and my parents' home, especially in spring. The road wound through farmland, hills, valleys and along a river for many miles. Beautiful lush green meadows, where the first young shoots of wheat were pushing through the fertile soil, were always so pleasing to the eye. I guess I should have called them paddocks! Don't you think meadows sound lovelier? Some of our Aussie words are so harsh compared to the English ones, like *creek*! Don't you think *stream* sounds so much gentler? So many of our vowel pronunciations in the 'Ocker' accent are so rough sounding, or as my Mum would say, uncouth! I often wonder how that even happened. Who's responsible, ha? Oh gosh, I'm off on another one of those detours, please excuse me! It's probably helping with all the memories of this particular day coming to mind, so I'll continue for just a tad longer.

Here is a line from a famous Australian folk song. Ohhh, how the words upset my ears, haha!

"There's a track winding back to an old fashioned shack."

Do you remember that one? I never warmed to it. I would rather be listening to, *"There's a lane winding along to a quaint little cottage!"* What? It doesn't rhyme? O.K., I'll move on now (she says with a bashful little smile! I would include an emoji here, but apparently that is not the 'done' thing in novels or the written word!).

Where was I? Oh yes. I do normally love this drive, but not on this particular day. I was fortunate enough to have one of the earlier models of hands-free phones installed in our car. What a help it was for this drive! I was able to talk to my sisters along the way, one who was able to get to the hospital before I was, and the other who had a longer drive than I, so was waiting to hear the news once we knew more.

The request of wanting to hear my Dad say **I love you** was paramount in my mind too. I prayed so hard, asking the Lord to please let Dad still be alive and to please give him the desire to tell me he loved me and my sisters too. I had convinced myself this would happen and God would keep Dad alive until my yearning desire was fulfilled. I had also convinced myself this was something Dad needed to say before he met his Heavenly Father, that somehow it was essential for his salvation. Of course, it was a totally misguided thought!

The hospital was on the farthest side of town, so I quickly found my way there, driving up and down familiar streets of my childhood years. It was a strange feeling, actually, as this was the hospital where I had endured three surgeries when I was growing up, and where I volunteered every Saturday for a few months while obtaining my Duke of Edinburgh Awards. Our house was only a block away, so the hospital was a building I saw every day for ten years of my younger life. As far as hospitals go, it was a lovely big pale brick building with beautiful gardens. In my stays there, and when I was allowed up and walking, I loved to go with my Mum when she visited, and we'd sit in the rose garden where there was an arched arbour.

(My Dad's departure.)

I parked the car and rushed through the door, to be greeted by a nurse who pointed me to what I presumed was the door I was to go through to see my Mum, sister, and whoever else was there waiting. Oh, how wrong I was. Dad was the only one in the room, laid out on a long, thin ambulance stretcher, still fully clothed, but he was definitely gone. The panic and sense of loss I felt was immense, for in that split-second moment I knew my request was lost forever. I wished I had not seen him gone from this world.

For many months after, I struggled with the scene of seeing my Dad deceased and wondered why God had allowed it. I never would have chosen to see him this way, not that he looked unpleasant at all; he actually looked quite at peace. It was just a sad reminder that my prayer had not been granted. For a long time afterwards, I voiced this to God! Being a very visual person, the image of him lying there upset me for many reasons of grief. But as time passed, and my prayers and questions were slowly answered, I started to see the beauty and purpose my Heavenly Father had in allowing me to be there.

It all came about in the form of a very special hymn, my Dad's favourite hymn. It amazed me how suddenly this song would be sung in church, be on *Songs of Praise* (a weekly viewing for me), and would even pop up on one of my husband's favourite gospel bands' videos. Sometimes I would even wake up singing it. When it came to mind, I would start to sing the meaningful words to myself, and over time God showed me a different way of seeing my dear Dad's departure. I will share with you the healed version of these moments, and hope in some way they will bless you and give you hope for those loved ones you have lost, and have wondered if they are at peace.

From my years growing up in the church, I feel it is often wrongly presumed that if a person isn't walking with the Lord in the way 'they' say they should, then they are lost forever and will never experience eternal life! As a child, I sat through many very fearful hell-fire-and-brimstone sermons of how God supposedly punishes us. It took many years for me to unlearn these teachings and relearn God's true character. He is righteous; holy; pure; perfect love; faithful; merciful; true; just; patient; kind; slow to anger; compassionate; and many more. Because we have our own free will, which gets us into all sorts of strife, it is God's merciful, patient discipline that saves us. Yes, He does discipline

His children when needed, but I don't believe He punishes us in cruel, horrid, abusive ways.

So in explaining all that, a Gentle Whisper I cling onto is that we never know what happens in one's final breaths of life, or the moments after. What I do know is that our all-knowing and compassionate Heavenly Father, who is very patient and kind, loves His children perfectly, and as the Bible says, 'does not want anyone to perish.' Meditating on another verse, Psalm 145:8-9, shows this so beautifully. King David wrote this Psalm after he had fallen into sin with Bathsheba, the wife of one of David's elite soldiers. Bathsheba became pregnant through this encounter. David then arranged for Uriah, her husband, to be moved to the frontline of battle, where he knew he would be killed. To be able to write such heartfelt and thought-provoking words after committing such a serious sin shows just how forgiving and loving the Lord is. The original King James Version paints a picture of God's character perfectly:

The Lord is gracious and full of compassion;

slow to anger and of great mercy.

The Lord is good to all; and His tender mercies

are over all of His works.

It is 30 years now since Dad left us. Some healings take what seems to be forever, but I have been walking in this new sense of letting go and peace for a few years now. It hasn't been a conscious sense of 'arriving' at this place of peace, but more a recognition that I am not unsettled anymore. That is one of the most beautiful things about some healings, especially those of the mind and emotions. It is as if a soft, gentle breeze has somehow floated by, taking all the troublesome thoughts with it. It shows me that God is always at work, even when we aren't aware of it. How reassuring!

Writing, re-writing, and debating whether I should even journal this story at all has been a dilemma in itself, but after I wrote the first edition of how that day affected me, I attended a concert at our church. And can you guess what was on the program? Yes, this most loving, soulful

Gentle Whispers

hymn, my Dad's favourite. I had only typed the events of that harrowing time the day before the concert, another Gentle Whisper that confirmed I must share how God has so tenderly brought me through to this awareness.

So this is how I now believe God planned the day of my Dad's passing:

The nurse pointed me to the door.

<u>*In the Garden*</u>

I come to the garden alone,

While the dew is still on the roses,

And the voice I hear falling on my ear

The Son of God discloses...

My Dad was no longer with us. There he was, alone in the dimly lit room, looking very peaceful, but I knew he wasn't there. I stood by his side, experiencing the strangest feelings I had ever encountered. It wasn't peace; it was more a numbness of my body, probably from the shock. It wasn't fear either, but a deep feeling of loss.

And He walks with me and He talks with me,

And He tells me I am his own;

And the joy we share as we tarry there,

None other has ever known...

Over time, as I have meditated on this scene with the Lord, it was almost a sense of inconceivable tranquillity as I gazed down at him. The Gentle Whisper that came to mind in that surreal moment was that I was witnessing something very significant, not only for my Dad but for me. To be honest though, at that time I would not have chosen this at all. Those unspoken words, *'I love you'*, were gone, heartbreakingly lost in an instant, never to leave his lips.

He speaks, and the sound of His voice is so sweet,

The birds hush their singing.

And the melody that He gives to me

Catherine Grace

Within my heart is ringing...

Disappointment was creeping into my thoughts, but I didn't become emotional. I have a deep understanding now that it wasn't my Dad's words to me that were needed most at that important moment, but God's words to my Dad. I remember speaking a prayer over Dad, still not fully knowing what was taking place, but I didn't touch him at all. The thought that I would be interrupting something very special between Heavenly Father and His son became very clear to me.

I'd stay in the garden with Him,

Tho' the night around me be falling;

But He bids me go, thro' the voice of woe,

His voice to me is calling.

I do believe that God was there with my Dad in that hospital room, calling his name. The fullness of that encounter I will never know, but I do know that my Dad was in his beloved garden with his Lord. The rest isn't mine to know. It is a precious and private moment between God the Father and His precious child.

And He walks with me and He talks with me,

And He tells me I am his own;

And the joy we share as we tarry there,

None other has ever known...

"In the Garden"

C. Austin Miles 1865 – 1946

I left the room with thoughts of my Mum and sister. Where were they? Had they seen Dad before he passed away? Did they know that he was gone? Were they still waiting for the doctor to come? All these questions were soon to be answered, but what a blessing it was for me to know he was in the garden.

I am forever grateful I was given this moment of insight and understanding. Over time, and when I was ready, God enabled me to view those last moments in a different light, in a way that would give me peace. I'm so grateful my eyes were opened to the fact that my Dad was worthy of his favourite song; that his last breaths were with Jesus, who made it all possible through His sacrifice, a belief that Dad held onto throughout all the turmoil he endured during his life.

Worthy of every song we could ever sing

Worthy of every praise we could ever bring

Worthy of every breath we could ever breathe

We live for You, oh, we live for You.

Jesus, the name above every other name

Jesus, the only One who could ever save

Worth of every breath we could ever breathe,

We live for you, we live for you.

From

Build my Life

Housefires – Worshiptogether.com Songs.

There are so many personal songs I have held onto over the years, songs that bring meaning and hope in times of need, but the above one was playing on Spotify's *Best of Live Worship* (a playlist I listen to often when I'm home) when I finished the revised version of my Dad's story. It has become a favourite, and another Gentle Whisper confirmed to my heart.

As the years roll on, there have been times when the Lord has led me in His love to those around me, mostly elderly people who are troubled about the ones they have lost. Like me, they have probably been subject to those frightening hell, fire and brimstone sermons! I do hope with all my heart that those of you who have had similar doubts or moments like mine, and have 'wondered' about your dearly departed ones, can know too that God never leaves us or forsakes us, no matter what we have done in our lives, and definitely not even in our last moments. Like the hymn says, *'His voice to me is calling and He tells me I am His own.'* No matter what people's lives have been like, we can never know their last thoughts, what happens in their final breaths, or what takes place after. If we really think about it, who would turn away from the most perfect love you could ever imagine? Please don't be tormented by harmful notions, but let them go to a loving God who only wants the best for all His children. Remember that Jesus is always calling your name too. Be at peace!

The days following Dad's passing were probably what you would call surreal, with family, extended family, and friends coming and going. Planning the graveside and memorial services with Mum and my sisters kept my mind off everything else, really. It wasn't until about a month later, when things were settling down and reality was setting in, that those thoughts of the lost words *'I love you'* really started to play on my mind again. Quiet times with the Lord, reflecting on seeing my Dad gone from this world, were difficult as I mulled over what I felt was a huge loss. Surely it wasn't too much to ask, was it? Surely every daughter should hear those precious words *'I love you'* from their father at least once in their life, shouldn't they? Well, of course they should, at least most days, actually!

My daily devotional flip-over calendar stood on the kitchen windowsill. Each day, I was usually very meticulous about reading each verse and inspirational thought, but since Dad's passing, I wasn't particularly interested in what it had to say. I wasn't angry with God, but was more filled with disappointment and confusion. I just didn't understand. The God of the universe, who is so magnificently great and wonderful, the creator of all things, the one who gave His Son to take away the sins of the world, why hadn't He allowed me to hear those most precious words I had longed to hear for so long? Why had I had to see him gone with no hope?

It was as if the devotional was calling me with the familiar Gentle Whisper. *No, not today, thank you!* I even moved it down toward the corner of the windowsill so it wasn't in full view when I looked out to see our beautiful back garden, oh, the garden, my Dad's favourite hymn. The last time I had heard him sing this hymn was when he surprised us all with a rendition at his 70th birthday party in front of many family and friends. As I gazed out at the alluring view, the words of the old hymn started playing in my thoughts, and soon I was humming the tune. Before I could even think of changing my mind, the devotional was in my hands. The Gentle Whisper had taken over my thinking without me even realising. I flipped over to the date of Dad's passing and started reading the inspirational thought:

> *"Why do you concern yourself*
> *with all the prayers you*
> *think God hasn't answered.*
> *Leave them to Him and be*
> *grateful for all the prayers*
> *He has answered!"*

It was the second time I had shed a tear since Dad's passing. The first time was in a shop when I saw a little golden trumpet Christmas decoration. You may remember my Dad was a wonderful trumpet player. Tears had not come easily, there were too many unanswered questions, but on these two occasions, they certainly did. My eldest, like-minded niece had given me this devotional calendar book the Christmas before. I wonder what was in her thoughts when she chose it. Well, knowing what we do know about being prompted by those gentle whispers, I'm sure she heard, *'choose this one!'*

The days that followed were filled with comfort and healing. The Gentle Whisper from above in one little verse was far more restoring than I could have imagined. This verse brought with it an understanding of what I had experienced in the dimly lit room with my Dad that day. He definitely 'wasn't there'. He was in *'The Garden'*, experiencing first-hand the perfect love from his Heavenly Father, who was waiting with open arms to greet him in his final breaths. Oh, how I love this scene, my Dad, with his arms open wide to meet his Abba Father, who knew and so mercifully understood and forgave all of my Dad's shortcomings. God knew the reasons why: the harsh and cruel childhood he had endured; his time in the war, fighting in the Middle East, Darwin, and Papua New Guinea; the war neurosis (now diagnosed as Post-Traumatic Stress Disorder) he suffered dreadfully for the rest of his life. Yes, God did see it all and wanted more than anything to heal His beloved son completely and perfectly. And what better place than with the hymn my Dad had loved so dearly? No wonder gardens are my most favourite place to be. I feel so divinely fortunate to have been able to share those last few moments with my Dad. I came to understand over time that he was *'In the Garden'*, and God so gently and perfectly was caring for my needs as well. I don't think I will ever doubt the healing powers of a garden:

> *The kiss of sun for pardon.*
> *The song of the birds for mirth.*
> *One is nearer God's heart*
> *in a garden,*
> *than anywhere else on earth.*
> *Dorothy Frances Gurney, 1858 – 1932*

It certainly is lovely to know that I am not the only one with these beliefs. During the time of writing all these thoughts down, I was watching another *Songs of Praise* programme late one Sunday evening. I pricked up my ears when I heard they would be visiting a garden in the medieval area of Duddingston, just outside Edinburgh.

Duddingston Kirk (church) on the shores of Duddingston Loch dates back to 1145. It wasn't until the 1960s that parish attendees Andrew and Nancy Neil, who were general practitioners in the area, had the thought to transform the beautiful surroundings of the church into a garden of serenity and peace. Over the years, many volunteers have helped bring this garden to life, not only physically but spiritually too, as prayer seems to surround its very existence. Some of these gardeners' insights were thought-provoking, and the analogies so helpful if we apply them to our own lives.

These thoughts were timely for me while sharing my stories here with you.

> *"It's during times of connecting with each other*
> *like the plants in a garden do as they intermingle,*

you can see that they are propping each other up."

"People come to the garden and learn from nature –

It's when we are pruning or cutting back that we

realise we become stronger."

"It is through the beauty of a garden that we

can fully see that this is where The Holy Spirit is."

The Reverend Jim Jack, the current minister at Duddingston Kirk, finished this programme with a heartfelt prayer.

"Lord, may our hearts

be open to the

beauty that

glows bright in the world

around us."

What better place for this to happen than in a garden? I hope that, through the connection of this book, you are feeling a little propped up and becoming stronger, as some of those old thoughts are being cut back and pruned. Is there a garden nearby where you can go for a wander? Wouldn't that be lovely? Off you go. I'm sure the Holy Spirit has some beautiful gentle whispers to share with you right now, guiding you to a place of serenity and peace.

Reflections: In the months and years that have followed, I am so blessed that God has also given me the ability to forgive my Dad. There have been many instances where I have offered up thoughts towards heaven and let them go with a prayer of *'I forgive you, Dad'*. I love raising my hands towards a twinkling starry night, to give and also to receive what is there waiting for me.

"Oh Lord, you know me so well.

You know everything about me;

where I am whether awake or asleep;

my thoughts, whether good or bad;
even what I am about to say,
before I say it!
You are with me every second of every day
and cover me with your blessings,
no matter where I am in the world.
It is such an inconceivable thought,
that there is nowhere that I
can hide from you.
And Lord, I would never want to!
You are my morning, noon and night
and how awesome it is to know,
the darkness cannot hide
your face from me,
It will be as the stars that shine
more brightly in the deep of the night."

C.G. – My thoughts as I read from Psalm 139:1-12

Each time, whether in the day or at night, when I have forgiven, not only my Dad but other wrongdoings I have endured, I have received far more love than I could have ever hoped or dreamed of. Love can come in many forms: a tangible gift; a beautiful sight in nature; someone else speaking those three precious words to me. Other times it has been a knowing in my spirit that Heaven is smiling down on me, like those twinkling stars at night.

During these moments, I must remember that I also need to ask for forgiveness, from God, from those I have sinned against, and also from myself. How can I ever expect to be free in the area of forgiveness if I don't deal with it in my own life first? It is all very well to say *'I forgive others'*, but when I haven't even stopped to ask for forgiveness myself, what is the point? Gentle Whispers are such a precious friend at these times. To know that God is with me, keeping me humble and prompting me when needed, is a gift that keeps pride away. Repentance is not a very comfortable or popular word, but if we want to see *"His Kingdom come on Earth as it is in Heaven"* or to have eternal life, it is something we are all going to need to do. Thank God for His amazing grace, patience, and long-suffering, and thank God there is no condemnation in any of this, just perfect love.

A confirming Bible verse I came across not long after my Dad had passed says it all:

> *The Lord your God is with you,*
>
> *The Mighty Warrior who saves.*
>
> *He will take great delight in you;*
>
> *He will quieten you with His love*
>
> *And take away your fears.*
>
> *He will rejoice over you with singing.*
>
> *Zephaniah 3:17 NTL*

He will take great delight in me. He quietens me with His love, yes, He loves me. He takes away my fears. He rejoices over me with singing, even though I am not perfect and never will be (well, not in this life anyway). What more could I ask for? There have been many times in my life since first coming across this verse that it has shown itself in the most heartfelt ways. Cards from friends, where this verse has been written at just the right moment when a hug from Heaven has been needed, are the most healing gifts of love I could ever receive. There have also been many songs based on this verse written over the years.

One such song came in the most special of circumstances. We were at our grandson's Grandparent Day, all assembled in an outdoor covered area between the classrooms. The dear little children all walked in and seated themselves on the floor in front of the grandparents on mats that were set out for them. They looked so tiny and very cute in their school uniforms. Heads were continually bobbing up and down, turning around with the hope of seeing their Grandma and Grandpa sitting behind them. Yes, there he was, waving frantically until we responded.

The first items on the agenda were some songs. We were all invited to stand and join in with the words on the screen at the front. The first song was very boppy, with fun-filled actions where the grandparents were asked to join in. Of course, Granny and Pops obliged! The next song was one we hadn't heard before. The scene that followed will stay with me forever. These beautiful little children were all standing there with their arms reaching to Heaven, singing the most touching words. The lyrics of the song were obviously meaningful not only to Pops and me but also to the other grandparents, as there was hardly a dry eye, it was such a tender moment!

I'll leave them for you to ponder, with this thought: I wonder if I would have been open to these most comforting experiences if I hadn't forgiven all those offences that have come against me over the years. I believe with all my heart that forgiveness is the key to an open Heaven over our lives. Unforgiveness can certainly be a blockage, or a wall we put up, which sadly can prevent us from receiving all God has waiting for us. Notice I said *'we put up'*! Of course, God's mercies and grace are perfect and always there for us, but it is us who can stop the blessing by our attitudes and reactions.

If you do struggle to forgive, try raising your hands and reaching them to Heaven and ask Jesus to help you. He is longing to make it as easy for you as He can with His perfect love. My prayer for you is that you will hear or sense the Gentle Whisper of your Heavenly Father singing over you, there is nothing more healing and lovely!

<u>Song of my Father</u>

When silence falls

I hear you call

In the secret place

You still my soul

With quiet joy

Gentle Whispers

And I'm wide awake
Chorus – In the middle of the night
I look up to the sky
I can hear you
Singing over me
Through the fire and the flood
I know that I am loved
I can hear you
Singing over me, yeah

You spoke the earth
With just one word
And you hold my heart
Oh, my every step
My every breath
Is your work of art
Chorus
I hear Your melody
I hear Your symphony
There's nothing louder than the song of my Father
I hear Your melody
I hear Your symphony
There's nothing louder than the song of my Father
By
Urban Rescue, Wild Heart album, 6 May 2016

Catherine Grace

Footnote: It was Mother's Day when I had finished writing and re-writing this chapter, such is the life of a fastidious writer. My birthday is exactly a month before Mother's Day, and as our family was not able to get together for my birthday, we arranged to meet at a favourite beachfront café to celebrate both occasions. To say I was delighted with the most thoughtful gift is quite an understatement. Is there a word for *over-delighted*? Well, that was me!

As I carefully prized the wrapping paper from the gift, a framed picture revealed individual flowers, each with the names of my family members on them. When gathered together, it resembled a beautiful garden. Each member of our family had their own flower: my three children, their wives and partner, our grandchildren, my husband and I each had flowers that bloomed during the month of our births. The script underneath the flowers said *'Granny's Garden'*.

What also made this so special is that no one in my family knew I was writing another book, and certainly did not know of this chapter. All will be revealed at just the right time, but how remarkable this Gentle Whisper is. The heart-warming gift sings over me now every time I gaze at it!

Gentle Whispers

Home is where your heart takes you.....

Catherine Grace

Chapter Five: Home Sweet Home

Mid pleasures and palaces

though we may roam,

be it ever so humble,

there's no place

like home.

John Howard Payne

9 June 179 –10 April 1852

We love visitors coming to our garden, especially the furry and feathered variety. Oh, does that sound like I don't appreciate the human kind? Of course, I do, and we are often encouraged with kind and complimentary words about our garden, but when the animal variety comes, we really do get excited! Like this week, when a brush-tailed possum took up residence in one of the birdhouses my hubby made a couple of years ago. Our grandson was staying with us when we first saw the dark brown, bushy tail poking out of the round hole that was meant for a bird to nest in. There was great excitement! We didn't mind in the least. How thrilling to have a little Australian native animal wanting to make our weeping ficus tree its home.

Over the years, in the many gardens we have had, one of the first jobs on the agenda has always been to get cracking in the garden to make it lush, colourful, and beautiful. That's when we really feel like it's home. Both our mums loved gardening, and we always include some of their favourites. My mum loved sweet little heartscases. They belong to the viola family, and their yellow and purple faces really do bring a smile. She also loved pansies, and as she aged and the task became too tiresome, we would help her plant around Easter time when the weather was cooling. I can't wait to get to the nursery each year to make my choices, not only in memory of Mum but also because they really are the happiest little flowers I know. Their colours are so bright and cheery, you can't help but smile. I prefer to buy the potted colour so the blooms are ready to open as soon as their roots hit the soft, fertile soil we've prepared for them. Heartseases are hard to find now in potted colour or seedlings, so we search for packets of seeds and scatter them around, loving the surprise of where their happy little faces pop up.

My hubby's mum's favourite bush was the Cecile Brunner rose (Rosa 'Cecile Brunner'). This delightful, delicate rose was first bred in France in the 1800s. It is an heirloom variety with posy-like pale pink blooms and a soft, sweet fragrance. The flowers are a favourite for bridal bouquets. Where I am seated typing this book, I can look to my right, out the window, and see Cecile Brunner in full flower right now. Oh, she is beautiful, with her long stems reaching to the very top of the garden wall. The floribunda variety, also called cluster-flowered roses, means we can have up to five or six blooms on the end of each stem. They tend to be repeat-flowering roses right through summer and into autumn. What a joy to have these dear little buds in our gardens over the years, in the many homes we have lived in.

I wonder what makes you feel right at home. Sometimes, as I write, I wish we could sit and chat together over a lovely cup of tea (I'll have Earl Grey with a splash of almond milk, thank you, what will you have?) about the things that touch your heart. But here you are, having to just listen or read what I have to say. Oh, poor you, but I do genuinely wonder such things. Having lived in many homes over my life, I have had so many varied experiences of what makes a house a home, and I know you would have too. Maybe some of my thoughts will bring lovely musings back to your memory. I hope so.

Sadly, in the world today, some unfortunate people don't even have the experience of a safe roof over their heads. There are currently 123,000 people without homes in this country. How heartbreaking and devastating is that! The fastest-growing group of homeless people in this country at the moment is older women. That was such a shock to read. I am an older woman, and I can't even imagine not having a home to go to, a comfortable bed to lie in, a kitchen to make a lovely cup of tea, a lounge chair to sit back in and watch my favourite TV show, or a shower at the end of the day to feel clean and refreshed before I slip between the sheets. No garden either, to take a moment during my busyness, gather my thoughts, and talk to Jesus as I thank Him for each bloom. I cannot imagine that, yet there are so many who live this way.

"Lord Jesus,

please bring an answer to the

powers that be who can do something

to bring this homelessness to an end!

Please put strategies and funding in place.

Show us how we can help and take away

all selfishness and greed.

Please be with each person who doesn't have a home!

Touch them deeply to meet their every need.

In the midst of their hopelessness, comfort them

with your love and may they turn to you–

the one who is their future and hope.

In Jesus' name,

Amen."

Thank you for joining me in praying this prayer. Each one of us can do something, even if it is just praying for these helpless people. I am reminded of a beautiful friend I had for many years. Sadly, she left us for her heavenly home way too soon, God knows. The gift of generosity and care came so naturally to her. Have you ever heard the term *"an angel without wings"*? Well, that was this dear lady, who now has her wings.

It was not unfamiliar to find this gentle soul sitting in the back row of church with another of her newly found unfortunate friends. On Sunday mornings, she would arise early and go for a walk or drive, praying that God would show her where to find the person He wanted her to bless. She certainly had the ability to hear His Gentle Whispers. It didn't happen every week, but many times there the needy one would be, as if waiting for the divine appointment God had set up for her. Leonie would take her home, run a bath, feed her breakfast, and then offer to take her to church. Sometimes she would share her wardrobe too, to help the person feel fresh and loved. More often than not, the offer was accepted, which began a road to recovery for this dear one who didn't have a future. When the situation seemed appropriate and safe, and she could see it was truly a sign of what God wanted, she would offer them a room in her home until they could get back on their feet. What a woman! I admired this beautiful soul so much. Her quiet and almost reserved ways didn't seek attention or acknowledgement for what she was doing, but I know the day she was given her wings, all Heaven was there waiting with open arms to receive her and applaud the selfless life she lived here on earth.

Sometimes you just need a sign.

When you need an answer and direction for a very important decision you have to make, do you ever wish Heaven would drop a sign down from the sky saying, "Go this way," or "No, don't do that, do this instead"? I certainly do, and I'm even well known in my family and circle of friends for asking for a sign! Haha, I can even hear it echoing now, "Ooo, it must be a sign," spoken to me in jest! Well, for me, it's easy. If I don't know what to do, I know God does, and He gave us His Holy Spirit for moments just like this. Yes, I do believe in the Father, Son, and Holy Spirit, and what does the Bible say about the Holy Spirit and who He is:

God also testified to it by signs,

wonders and various miracles,

and by gifts of the Holy Spirit distributed

according to His will.

Hebrews 2:4 NIV

And also Jesus' words before He ascended to Heaven:

Whoever believes and is baptised

will be saved...

Catherine Grace

and these signs will accompany
those who believe…
and the Lord worked with them
and confirmed His word by the signs
that accompanied it.
Mark 16:16–20

Now, who is going to argue with that? I hope it doesn't sound a tad too preachy. I do need to make a point so it is believable and not just Cathy on another one of her eye-rolling *"it's a sign"* moments! All throughout the Good Book are stories of kings, prophets, disciples, and everyday people being given signs from above to lead and guide them, to show them what to do next, and even to warn them of the consequences if they made a wrong decision. So, let's continue with this little *spiro* and quite an unbelievable story. You can believe me, it did happen, and it was definitely a Gentle, yet much stronger than normal, Whisper that came in the form of a sign, and it happened to my husband!

I have struggled with how much to share about this story for the sake of protecting the innocent and not judging the guilty, that is God's job! Many words have been changed, and re-editing of each paragraph has taken place, but in the end, I want to be truthful without throwing spears. I know there have been many senior employees treated this way over the years, so knowing that you are not alone may help too, especially when you hear how God does intervene and brings hope and healing to any situation.

We were in quite a dilemma. It was at a time in history when some businesses were not treating employees close to retirement justly. I won't go into detail, but through no fault of their own, many started disappearing from these companies in their sixties, with my hubby being one of them. Two days after he lost his job, there was a photo in the paper advertising the new direction this company was taking, along with a picture of their brand-spanking-new, young employee who would meet all their requirements. We were devastated! What was worse was that these businesses had found ways to 'legally' remove employees who had not only worked so hard for them for years but had also sacrificed greatly, with long hours and endless effort, to keep their employers happy.

Hubby explored many avenues of counsel and help but was shocked to find he had missed the cut-off point for being able to appeal his dismissal. They had forgotten to tell him that detail! The feeling of loss, abandonment, and betrayal was huge. Hubby felt strongly that he was to go to court to try to bring light to what was happening and to plead his personal case. Three court cases later, and with a negative result, it wasn't all wasted, as other workers in the same position took their stand, and we soon saw these unfair rules change. There was also an inquiry into what these businesses were doing, and appropriate action was taken. Sadly, though, our loss was great. Isn't it dreadful when employees become a dollar sign rather than a human being with needs for their retirement and the years ahead?

We prayed and prayed, even on our knees! Little by little, we saw the hand of our Heavenly Father working for us in miraculous ways. We sold our very large home, held garage sales, and went to markets to sell some of our belongings. Who would have thought downsizing could be fun? We also decided to pull back on eating out, expensive social activities, and travel for a while. Yes, life was very different, but we knew that what we were experiencing was, in weird and wonderful ways, good for us and, of course, for God's glory.

During the six months of living on long service leave, doing odd jobs that caring friends offered my husband, and running my art classes and high teas in the studio, we grew closer together. We even started to see the benefits of living a simpler life, and the thought of moving to a smaller home didn't faze us, even if it was ten years earlier than we had planned. Gentle Whispers were comforting and frequent during this time through our devotions, prayer, and beautiful, faithful friends and family. People who had been through the same experience were brought across our path, and times of sharing and encouragement were deeply healing.

I remember one very special encounter at our local shopping centre, where I loved to browse. I find "just looking" so therapeutic. Gazing at beautiful things and seeing how they are made brings me so much joy. On such a browsing day, a lady who looked familiar came over and said she thought she knew me. After talking for a little while, we realised we had a mutual friend. This dear lady asked if I would like to join her and her husband at a nearby coffee shop. I was a little puzzled but accepted her kind offer.

During the next few minutes, which turned into two hours, the husband explained, after I asked about his work, that he had just lost his job. The circumstances were exactly the same as my hubby's. It was a different position, but the story was identical. This dear man was in his mid-sixties, like my hubby, had been in this line of work for many years, was looking forward to retirement, and then had the rug pulled out from under his feet. He was in the process of seeking legal action, using the support and knowledge that the government was encouraging employees to stay working until the age of seventy. When I asked the lady why she had approached me, she replied that she thought I looked a little lonely and was sure she knew me.

How beautiful is it that sometimes we respond to Gentle Whispers without even realising we are doing so, or why. After sharing our stories, I promised I would pray for them and their situation. Somehow the burden seemed to lift, and they too were grateful for our meeting, so much so that they insisted on paying for my coffee and meal. We were so grateful for these encounters that came through friends who were caring and helpful.

One of hubby's closest friends encouraged him that he could see him working in property, so off he went to do a Real Estate Property Management course in the city, about two hours from our home. It helped his self-esteem and eased his boredom. If you know my man, you will know that any excuse for a train ride is perfect.

One of the most precious things is when friends who are praying for you also hear the Gentle Whispers. On one particular day, a dear friend we had known since our teenage years rang to say she had seen an advertisement for a Property Manager at a local school. Well, it wasn't quite what we had in mind, but since it was for a Property Manager, hubby sent off an application and then had the thought, a Gentle

Gentle Whispers

Whisper of course, to send his résumé to other local schools, thinking that an outdoor, hands-on job was just what he needed.

Within a couple of days, he received a phone call, not from the advertised position, but from another school that had just opened his letter and résumé, enquiring about him for a job. Unbeknown to him, this school had also been advertising for the very same position but had not yet found someone suitable, so he was applying for a job he didn't even know existed. During the interview, many things were revealed; one being that this was the last day of his long service leave we needed to live on! That was a God surprise as we did not know what we would do after this, but He did!

Praise the Lord, he got the job and started the next day! We still needed to sell our home and find somewhere suitable to live for the remainder of our lives, hopefully. Ten previous homes were certainly enough, and the thought of this being short-term accommodation was just too much to bear after the stressful time we had been through.

We searched high and low, but after all our bills were paid off, we were limited in what we could afford. A little cottage somewhere quiet would be nice, or even a flat or townhouse where we could walk down the street for a coffee, that was another lovely thought. The search became quite fun, and as we narrowed the list down, one such place looked promising. We paid a holding deposit and had a deadline for Thursday afternoon at 4 pm to confirm we would buy this home.

One of the requirements at the school was for hubby to be a bus driver for the excursions the children would go on. Thankfully, he had acquired his bus-driving licence years before. This particular Thursday, it was a trip to the Museum in Sydney. Even with all the praying and asking for confirmation to purchase this property, we still weren't one hundred per cent sure this was the one for us. I rang my husband before he boarded the bus and said (of course she did), "Pray for a sign! We really do need a sign! We have to be out of our home by settlement in six weeks' time, so we need to know where to go."

Catherine Grace

All day, as I went about my daily tasks and hubby was driving the bus, we both prayed for God's grace and favour to show us a sign as to whether we should take this property or not.

The day sped by, and four o'clock was getting closer and closer. Then the phone call came in a rather shaky voice. "You won't believe this! Are you sitting down? Do you think this could be the sign?"

On the journey home with the bus full of children, something rather unusual happened. Driving up the freeway behind the school bus came a semi-trailer. He was in a terrible hurry, and even though the school bus was in the middle lane, this truck decided to pull out and overtake. What was he thinking? Hubby slowed the school bus down so the truck didn't have to break any speed limits and to make sure the children were completely safe. Then, as if to get the bus driver's attention, the truck driver pulled back into the middle lane in front of the bus.

Hubby was quite alarmed and, although he knew everything was safe, he wondered what on earth this crazy truck driver was doing. The truck didn't speed away but sat at an easy pace and continued on for quite a while in front of the bus. It wasn't long before hubby saw it. On the back of the long trailer, on both the left-hand and right-hand sides just above the wheels, was the name of the company the truck belonged to. Would you believe it? The name was the same as the housing estate where the home was, the one we needed to give our reply to at four o'clock that day.

And then he asked, "Do you think it's a sign?" Oh, I do love it when God amuses us so perfectly with exactly what we need to know. Needless to say, we made the meeting, and we even told the salesperson our rather miraculous and unique story about the "sign" on the back of a semi-trailer that helped us make up our minds. She was very impressed, saying all our stars were aligned at that moment. Bless her.

I'd love to be able to say it has all been smooth sailing in our new home, but as we all know, life isn't all fairy floss and roses, is it? It can be said, though, that God has used many of the issues we've had in our home, which flooded many times and wasn't compliant with council, to bring to light the underlying problems affecting other properties around us.

Gentle Whispers

Each home will end up being completely rebuilt and compliant with council regulations, at no cost to the owner. Our place is finished now, and it is such a lovely home to live in.

We have a beautiful, relaxing back courtyard and walled garden where our Cecile Brunner rose grows among other pretty plants and flowers. I'm very excited to see the new buds forming on the hollyhock we have planted there. The colours will be a complete surprise.

About the walled garden, the Gentle Whisper was so beautiful when we first saw this courtyard at the back of the home we were purchasing. I had read it in a devotional just a few days before:

My holiness is to

have a wall around

your garden; a wall of protection

and blessing.

Why do I ever doubt the abundant, kind, and wonderful provision of my Heavenly Father? Sometimes it doesn't happen the way we anticipate. There are plans and purposes to live through first. To have a lovely new room to paint in, where ladies can come and share the joy and appreciation of creating beautiful artworks, and also a sunroom to relax in, is life-giving.

To be able to stop and listen to the pitter-patter of rain when it falls, and not be in dread of another flood, is such a gift we appreciate so much. It didn't happen straight away, but we can be so grateful for God's leading and wisdom, which were not only for ourselves but for others in our area who needed a helping hand to be able to call where they live *Home Sweet Home*.

Home isn't your living room;

It's not even your street or town.

Home is what you feel–

It's where your heart takes you!

—Robson Green, *Walking Hadrian's Wall* (2021)

Catherine Grace

Reflections: Gentle Whispers and signs were definitely a part of this journey, not just for us but for others whom God involved along the way to bring about His will, plans, and purpose for all our good. Never underestimate the gift your voice, words, prayers, and encouragement can be to others as you stand up for what is right. You just may be part of the huge change needed for their rescuing and healing, leading them to their future and hope.

A well-known Aussie saying is "she'll be right, mate" or "it's just life," often said with a shrug of the shoulders. Well, can I expand your thinking a little before I go any further, as to what I think about these rather empty sayings? My aim here isn't to offend anyone or brush aside any grief or hurt you may be going through, so just humour me a tad and let me explain. There are four very important words I live by that bring so much clarity, understanding and meaning to my life: reasons; seasons; plans; purposes. You have just been reading about these words in the previous stories. Well I'll phrase it this way:

There are reasons for the seasons

you are in,

for God's plans and purposes

to be revealed.

C.G. '24

Whether or not you are among the 78 per cent of people who, like the Greek philosopher Aristotle, believe that everything happens for a reason, there is value in exploring this theory. It is not up to me to judge whether Aristotle believed in the true God, Creator of the Universe, but I find it helpful and comforting to know that God knows and can be with me in the process of all life's events. He can bring confirming God surprises and Gentle Whispers to those who desperately need clarity and closure in their situations.

It can also come down to a certain personality trait, especially if you are like a sniffer dog or you must have all your little ducks in a row, like "mwah," she says with a wink, just love me anyway!

Straight away, I know this can bring up all sorts of arguments and questions, especially if the circumstances you have been through have been traumatic and hurtful. Sometimes it is just too difficult to look for the reason, as this can bring blame and confusion, especially if it is at the hands of someone else or when your grief has been too hard to bear.

I don't believe God is to blame for these hardships. Remember, we live in a fallen world, with each person having free will. God does grieve with us in these situations, and the Word says that Jesus wept over many sad situations in people's lives. What I can say, though, is that it is during these times of hardship that I am encouraged to dig deeper, to search my soul, to find out who I really am, who my fellow man is, and most importantly, who God is in the midst of it all.

During these reflective times, I am always reassured that God is in control, no matter the circumstances. What may look dreadfully wrong and sometimes cruel to us can be completely put right by Him, who has all the pieces of the puzzle ready to fit together, piece by piece. He is the one who will rescue us from our dilemmas and bring healing, love, and victory to our lives.

Be kind to yourself, though. If your brain is in overload and it all seems too much, please don't put yourself under pressure. All we need to do, until we are stronger, is to trust Him and rest in His loving arms, especially if our minds aren't yet able to fathom our situation. In the meantime, be assured that God is with you, and there will come a time to gain understanding and closure. It is sometimes helpful to remember this comforting verse too, from God's Word:

> *I have told you these things,*
>
> *so that in me, you may have peace.*
>
> *In this world, you will have trouble.*
>
> *But take heart, I have overcome the world!*
>
> John 16:33

'She'll be right, mate' thinking certainly isn't going to do me any favours either. In the depths of our despair, nothing seems right, but there is One who can make it right. I don't think the saying is meant to be harmful, but it can reflect a rather apathetic outlook on the dramas of life. 'It's just life' isn't going to give us any answers either. I find it such a hollow and flippant statement, often said after something bad or unfortunate has happened, to express the feeling that such events occur and we just have to accept them.

Well, this is where 'what if' is very helpful. What if we don't have to accept them? What if we don't have to live with them? What if there is an answer if we would only dig a little deeper? What if there is someone who can turn the situation around and make it right again? What if complete healing, restoration, and victory are there waiting for us to reach out and take them? That is a lot of 'what ifs', but in believing there are reasons for the seasons, and through prayer, soul-searching, and a little faith, isn't it worth the journey to find out what God's plans and purposes are?

There is a beautiful verse that shows the heart of God for each one of us. He has seen everything that has happened to you. Because of His most gracious, caring, and loving character, it hurts Him deeply to see how you have suffered. But because of our unalterable free will, He can't change it, although He can heal it and make all things new. That's why He sent Jesus, to take all of the dreadful things He knew would happen in this world and make them healed and whole again.

Jesus took it all: the pain, the torment, the hurt, the trauma, every sickness, every hardship, every sin, and everything sin causes. Oh, if only man would believe and apply it to their lives! *Apply* is the big word here too. We can't just look at it and expect everything to fall into place. We actually have to believe, to act, and to put into practice what is needed. So these are the plans God has for us all:

For I know the plans

I have for you,

declares the Lord.

Plans to prosper you and

not to harm you,

plans to give you a hope and a future.

Gentle Whispers

Jeremiah 29:11 NIV

There is a fact and truth we will all face, though, which is 'just life'. We are all going to leave this world one day. We are all going to find our wings. Someone we love dearly is going to say goodbye. In this fallen world, there will be seasons of hardship, deep loss, and grief. Ecclesiastes 3 explains them all clearly and completely, but for whatever reason you are in a particular season, be assured God is there to turn it all for your good. His plans are to prosper you and not to harm you.

Instead of saying 'it's just life', try exploring those moments a little deeper. I'm sure that's when you will find the hidden treasures of reasons for the seasons that bring about God's plans and purposes. Jeremiah 29:11 goes on to say in the following verses:

Then you will call on me

and come and pray to me,

and I will listen to you.

You will seek me and find me

when you seek me with

all your heart.

Jeremiah 29:12–13 NIV

It is so important to try not to give up, as hard as that might seem in the midst of it all. To know that not one drop of what you are going through will be wasted is such a precious truth. In the process, your Heavenly Father wants you to cling to Him while He wipes every tear and draws you closer to His healing and perfect love, as He fills you with hope for the future He has planned for you.

I often wonder where we would be if we hadn't looked a little deeper in our time of distress when hubby lost his job or when the home we thought would be our dream home ended up being a nightmare. If we hadn't given all of this to God to sort out the reasons for the season and what His plan and purpose were, I really do wonder what the outcome would have been. Would the caring friend have heard the Gentle Whisper to encourage hubby to get his Property Manager's Certificate?

In the end, it was for a different property manager's position, but at that time, it gave him a purpose to get out of bed every day, even if he didn't yet know the plans ahead. It filled him with hope and brought confirmation when the right Property Manager's job came along. It even brought a smile, especially for our friend who was sure the Gentle Whisper he heard was 'Property Manager'. Then there was the dear lady who spotted a job in the paper and passed it on. It wasn't the job that was meant for him, but it did put hubby on the right track and gave him the confidence to send out five other résumés, one of which was successful.

Digging deeper is often just what is needed. Then there were the dear friends who owned the property with many jobs needing to be done and who so generously knew hubby was the man for the job. He loved doing this work, and it ended up being the exact type of work he would be doing in his new position. What a perfect plan that was, with all the purposes revealed.

The list is endless for all these reasons, and we are so grateful for the prayers, phone calls, and gifts of money that came our way at just the right time. People who will stop to hear those Gentle Whispers and act on them really are what God so desperately needs in this world for His plans and purposes to be achieved. I do hope you are listening and are ready, willing, and able to pass those whispers on to the people who need them. Isn't it just wonderful to be a part of those amazing God surprises He is waiting to lavish on His children? So, won't you let God use your hardships to show how He can bring His purposes, miracles, and healing into every situation? God doesn't cause the pain, but He will heal it if you let Him.

One of the most beautiful verses that brought comfort during this journey was from a favourite Psalm written in a new translation:

The Lord is my best friend and my shepherd.

I always have more than enough.

Gentle Whispers

He offers a resting place for me in his luxurious love.
His tracks take me to an oasis of peace near the quiet brook of bliss.
That's where he restores and revives my life.
Psalm 23:1–3 TPT

I know you won't be at all surprised to hear that our home has a terraced garden (yes, terraced, remember my studio name?) and right at the bottom of the garden is a babbling brook. We call it the 'Brook of Bliss'. The water frolics and dances over the smooth rocks all the way down to a pond not far away. It can be reached by a beautiful walk through the middle of a foliage-covered path. The ducks and waterfowl that have made the pond their *Home Sweet Home* are such a delight to see, and who wouldn't appreciate these quacking, waddling friends who come to say hello so often? Yes, it truly is *Home Sweet Home!*

Life is all about
saying goodbye!

Catherine Grace

Chapter Six: Sounds of Goodbye

How lucky I am

to have something

that makes saying goodbye

so hard.

Winnie the Pooh,

A. A. Milne (1882–1956)

I guess it is safe to say there would not be a person on this earth who hasn't experienced the sadness of saying fond farewells or goodbyes. In most cases, goodbyes are a sorrowful occasion, even if they happen for a good reason. The feelings of loss and emptiness can even bring on a physical ache in the chest.

A delightful book I recently finished reading describes so beautifully, and with deeply felt emotion, how we can cope with having to say goodbye. The sentence that touched me was quite simple, but it went deep within, striking a chord with the goodbyes I've faced over my life. It revealed the key in one word: remembering.

"Because remembering is

the only way

to let the pain out of

your heart."

From–Silver Linings by Katrina Nannestad

What a beautiful thought. Memories are a very special and much-needed gift from Heaven above, allowing us to treasure the people, places and things we have had to say goodbye to. Remembering can bring joy as we think of the wonderful times we've had; the beautiful visions we've experienced of places we've seen and lived; the lovely possessions we've had to let go of; and, most of all, the love and attachment each of these has held for us, along with the many life lessons we've learnt along the way. Saying goodbye to pets really does break your heart too, and along with saying goodbye to precious family and friends, it would be the most difficult, even if it isn't forever.

I remember many occasions of being at the airport, waving off our three children as they set off on their overseas adventures. Oh, how that pulls at a mother's and father's heartstrings. The mixed emotions, excitement for the wonderful adventures ahead, yet the awareness that it may be months or even years before seeing them again, can be quite overwhelming, no matter how brave you try to be. The last impression you don't want to leave imprinted on your sons' and daughters' hearts is a mum who has lost the plot and is crying uncontrollably.

I do think I managed to spare them some awkwardness, but it certainly wasn't easy. Praise God for a quick exit to the car park after the final hugs were given and promises of keeping in touch and staying safe were made. Thankfully, over the years, all three, along with their wives, partner and children, have returned safely with marvellous stories to share, and a few souvenir gifts for us to display in our china cabinet and on our Christmas tree. Oh, they know their mother well.

Many films have been created around the theme of goodbyes, designed to draw deep emotion from the viewer. Producers know that goodbyes make money at the box office. Who could forget the dramatic and profound farewells in Gone with the Wind? There are several emotional and heartbreaking farewells to friends, family members and homes throughout this grand, award-winning film.

I'm sure you'll remember these parting words between Rhett and Scarlett in the final scene:

> *"Rhett, Rhett, where shall I go, what shall I do?"*
>
> *"Frankly my dear, I don't give a dam!"* Rhett says as
>
> *he disappears out the door and into the misty fog.*
>
> *"Oh, I can't let him go, I can't let him go!"* sobs Scarlett.
>
> *"There must be some way to bring him back,*

Catherine Grace

I'll think about it tomorrow! Sob, sob, sob!
Tara! I'll go home, I'll think of some way
to bring him back.
After all, tomorrow is another day!"
Gone with the Wind – novel by Margaret Mitchell, 1900 – 1949.
Production Companies: Selznick International Pictures, Metro-Goldwyn-Mayer 1939

Are you laughing or crying as the memories of this melodramatic moment come to mind? I must say I am having a little giggle now, but when I first saw it, I was sobbing along with poor Scarlett, who, in fairness, had brought much of the drama in her life upon herself.

And here's a thought... was it a Gentle Whisper Scarlett heard when she thought of returning to her beloved Tara? Did she think of a way to bring Rhett back? Oh, and the hope in knowing there is always tomorrow. I'll leave you to ponder these deep and meaningful reflections. I do wonder why they never made Gone with the Wind 2.

Another goodbye I had to endure a few years ago was when we left our previous home. I've mentioned that this forced move was quite challenging, and then came the downsizing that had to happen. Our system had to be ruthless, oh yes, very harsh and cruel, but there was simply no way the contents of a very large home were going to fit into a two-bedroom cottage.

We had three big boxes labelled: 'must keep', 'not keeping' and 'not sure yet'. When those three boxes were filled, we would start on the next three, continuing until everything was packed. Then came the 'not sure' boxes, the most difficult ones, because the 'not sure' almost always became 'sure'.

A painting I was very fond of was titled The Four Seasons of Mount Canobolas. It was painted in my realism decorative style, with the mountain and surrounding hills in the distance. The trees in the foreground included touches of autumn colour, of course, since our country town is proudly known as 'Colour City'. At the time, I truly

Gentle Whispers

couldn't believe we were leaving our beautiful autumn home, where the colourful leaves would float gently to the ground so faithfully each year. The painting held so much sentiment for me.

That reminds me of a poem I once wrote about my favourite season... now where is it? Ahhh, yes:

Leaves still fall

There's a chill in the air...
and nothing compares to the coolness that
comes after hot summer days.

Tranquil misty mornings...
of peaceful callings, to cool gentle breezes
and bright colour splendour.

Creation is resting...
a timely blessing, so raise hands to the
Heavens and release those cares.

A warm comfy rug...
curl up and get snug, yes it's time for calm rest
as your heart feels content.

Autumn leaves dancing...
bright colours singing, being lifted on angels'
wings carefree and light.

Catherine Grace

Remember the love…
that comes from above, and be eternally
grateful that Leaves Still Fall.

C.G. '08

To complete this painting, a garland was painted around the edge of fruits that were grown in the orchards on the foothills of this quite majestic mountain; native flowers which grew in our area; a Crimson Rosella perched on a gumnut blossom branch that was covered in snow; and of course those splendid autumn leaves. These all hugged the left-hand border, depicting the four seasons. I was very humbled to have been able to sell prints and cards of this scene in our local Information Centre for many years, until we moved to the coast, an idea I was given from another one of the most appreciated Gentle Whispers. Of course, the original was hung in pride of place in our new home after we moved to the coast.

When we were unpacking at our little home, I asked hubby if he had seen my painting of Mt Canobolas. He assured me it must still be in the garage waiting to be brought into the house. We searched the boxes but no painting. Where could it be? There were boxes of mostly china and Christmas decorations still to find a shelf or cabinet for, but sadly more culling was needed for these, yet none of them contained my painting. Then the thought came that it must have been accidentally placed in one of the 'not keeping' boxes by mistake.

We quickly drove to the charity shops we had donated these boxes to, but alas, no painting was ever to be found. At one of the shops they explained to us that most of their items are sent off in trucks to a centre many miles from us; another explained that if it wasn't in the shop, it must have been sold. So I convinced myself a holiday maker from our country town had purchased the painting and couldn't believe the luck of their find in a charity shop on the coast. Well, the thought did soften the blow just a tad.

Gentle Whispers

It wasn't until two years later that the most remarkable thing happened. Visitors from where we used to live were on the coast staying with other friends of ours. We were asked to join them for dinner, and over the course of the evening Wayne mentioned he had something he wondered if we would like to see, in the boot of his car. So off we went, wondering what on earth it could be. Would you believe it was a print of my 'Four Seasons of Mt Canobolas'?

Wayne was a Pastoral Carer at an aged care home in the town where my mum had lived. Years before, she had gifted her neighbour the painting, and now this dear soul had no further need of it as she was being moved to higher care. When Wayne inspected it, he knew that it was one of mine (well, under the circumstances I do believe it was a Gentle Whisper, don't you?). Knowing of my mum's and this lady's friendship, he decided to bring it over to the coast, wondering if I would like it. WOULD I? It now hangs in our sunroom, a place of peace, where we love to relax and unwind, as a constant reminder of just how loving and kind our Heavenly Father is. I do hope the owner of the original appreciates it as much as I do the print.

One of the most touching and meaningful goodbyes I know is when Jesus said His final farewell to His mother. I know I have mentioned this before in my writings, but the thought and love it brings to my heart is quite overwhelming, and a blessing for every mother, so I'll share it again… reminders can also be gentle whispers at just the right time.

It was such a devastating scene for all those who loved and followed Jesus. The Pharisee religious rulers who despised Jesus with jealousy and hatred thought they had finally won. Because of history and the written Word, we know they didn't. God's plan was fulfilled and is still being fulfilled today. Yet this moving scene of goodbyes was so distressing, but so meaningful. The Word says Mary the mother of Jesus, His aunt, Mary the wife of Clopas and Mary Magdalene stood at the foot of the cross:

When Jesus saw His mother and the disciple whom He loved standing beside her,

He said to His mother,

Catherine Grace

"Woman, here is your son."

Then He said to the disciple,

"Here is your mother."

And from that hour the disciple

took her into his own home.

John 19:26–27

I love The Passion Translation of these verses, which bring emotion and life to the depth of this last goodbye for His mother, whom He loved dearly, and the gentle words Jesus was able to whisper from the cross in His last breaths:

So when Jesus looked down and saw the disciple He loved standing with her,

He said, "Mother, look–John will be a son to you."

Then He said,

"John look–she will be a mother to you!"

From that day on, John accepted Mary into his home as one of his own family.

What hope that would have given Mary. Jesus, her beloved Son, was showing such care and compassion for her, even with the weight of the whole world on His shoulders. I'm also encouraged to know that throughout history and in the Word it is documented that John outlived Mary by many years. God's purpose for Mary being cared for until her passing was fulfilled. Surely this shows the depth of love God has for all mothers. I hope this little gentle whisper encourages those of you who need to know that today God is definitely also on the side of all women. Shame to those men over the centuries who have thought they were far superior!

My middle sister has not long returned from a trip to Turkey, Greece and Rome following the steps of the Apostle Paul. They visited Mary the mother of Jesus's home in Ephesus where she lived with John. It was so heart-warming to see the photos of this stone cottage where she lived safely and to remember Jesus's last words He spoke to His mother from the cross. They were words so filled with love that still move me to this day.

This next story includes all these things: purpose, God's unfailing love, signs, mothers and yes, goodbyes. My mum was always an instrument of peace in my life. She lived another 14 years after my dad passed away, and although she faced many challenges during the time that followed, I will always be grateful for the faith-filled wisdom, gentleness and peace she gave to me, and those who crossed her path, in those days.

Do you remember the dilemma we found ourselves in when we moved into our little downsize cottage? Well, here is a little more detail of Gentle Whispers and lessons we learnt during that time, and how God used my dear mum's gentle and quiet spirit even though I had said goodbye to her many years before.

Ulysses butterfly flutters

I couldn't believe my eyes. The window I was facing from inside our lounge room looked out to the front patio. We were in the middle of very serious talks with someone who was involved in the home we had just purchased, then as I looked over his shoulder a Ulysses butterfly fluttered right up to the window as if peering in.

Since moving into what we thought was going to be a peaceful time, we soon realised we couldn't have been more wrong. This move was supposed to be less work for us, with just a back courtyard and a front terrace garden to look after. Moving on from the dramas and sadness of having to sell our beautiful previous home and move away, all was looking quite rosy. Then the flood, and the next flood, and the next — well, this went on for six years. The main flow of this unwanted and frustrating water was right through the middle of my new studio. It seeped through to the second bedroom, and because of a leaking roof we also had waterfalls running down our inside walls. Outside, the current of water ran across our courtyard, through our garage, across the lane and down to our Brook of Bliss. Yes, the beautiful peaceful

Brook of Bliss that was supposed to be a confirmation that we were to live here.

Sadly, we were not the only ones in our area experiencing these problems, with some poor folk having lived here for years. Apparently, this area had long been known to have these sorts of issues, and even with our research and the signs pointing us to move here, it all seemed to have been kept from us until we experienced our first Niagara Falls flowing through our rooms. Our quaint little home (and others in the area) was a riverbed just waiting to be filled at any given moment from any torrential storm.

With many family and friends praying for us, we were still able to maintain the belief that God does not make mistakes. So we plodded on, trying to find the plan and purpose for our dilemma. It became quite apparent that other residents in our area were also working behind the scenes, trying to find answers. Some had already met with the local council but to no avail.

So came the meeting in our lounge room with the person we trusted and thought could help us. We prayed before he arrived, asking for guidance and of course a sign (God knows me well) and for some reason He chose the Gentle Whisper to be with wings, yes, a beautiful Ulysses butterfly. Why, you ask? How is it a sign? It's just a butterfly. Well, it was well known to me and my family that this was my mum's favourite butterfly. She simply loved them. Over the years she had taken photos of them on many trips with Dad, and she even asked me to paint one for her on a tray with her favourite native flowers.

Now, you don't have to worry about me because I don't think for a minute that Mum flew down from Heaven in the form of a bright blue Ulysses butterfly to tell me everything was going to be okay. But I do believe God used this wonderful creature to bring me peace, to settle my heart, and to show me He was fully aware of our situation and the dreadful situation others were in too. This butterfly isn't common in our area, and in the weeks that followed, this dear little flutterby appeared three more times at just the right moment, quite out of the blue, bringing us confirmation and peace. God knows us so well, doesn't He?

Gentle Whispers

Sometimes even at my age, a comforting thought or symbol of my peace-making mum is exactly what I need most.

One of those times was when my hubby and I were having a very dramatic (well, the drama was me) discussion about our future in this very sad and rather broken house. These times were so devastating, especially when flood after flood ruined more possessions, mostly things that were not replaceable. We thought we had everything moved up and out of harm's way, but the water just seemed to find them. Even photos of my previous studios and artwork were damaged beyond repair. Were the goodbyes ever going to end?

This time the Ulysses butterfly was fluttering around in our back courtyard where the walled garden was. It certainly stopped me in my tracks as I looked past my hubby's face and out the kitchen window. I pointed, and he too was amazed, firstly that a butterfly could stop my anxious and frustrated words, and secondly that this butterfly was actually enjoying our garden at that very moment. It stayed for just long enough for deep breaths to be taken and calmness to return.

The third time was when we decided we simply needed a coffee, hoping it would help bring some calm to our discussions. Have you ever had one of those moments? Neither of us is into stronger tonics that might have helped, especially not at 10 am, so coffee it was, as we really did need to make some very serious decisions about our future. A new coffee shop had opened in a new block of businesses not far away, so we decided to drive there. Our plan was to buy a takeaway and walk through the park to the waterfront, but once we arrived we loved the ambience of the outside area. It was quaint, with flower boxes and trees surrounding it. Even crammed between two new buildings, it had a lovely little city feel, like those charming alfresco dining spaces tucked away in CBD laneways.

Well, of course you know what delightful little creature found us in the middle of this cement city, don't you? There we were, sipping our lovely coffee and deep in discussion, when a bright blue Ulysses butterfly fluttered right between and around us for quite a few minutes. No more words were needed. We both sat there, simply enjoying the moment of awe and peace, knowing exactly what the answer was.

Catherine Grace

The good news is that everything has now been finished properly and to such a high standard. Everything is also fully compliant with council approval. It is so reassuring to know that there are still people in this world who are integral and do the right thing. We may not have enjoyed the whole scenario, but God knew this problem needed to be sorted not just for us but for others as well. Isn't it wonderful that He knows exactly where to shine His light and who to use to bring about the changes that are needed?

I'm reminded of this very helpful reading:

I have told you all this

so that you may have peace in me.

Here on earth, you will have

many trials and sorrows.

But take heart,

because I have overcome the world.

John 16:33 NLT

As for us? Well, of course you know we stayed. How could we leave our walled garden, our Brook of Bliss, our brand-new dry studio, and the assurance that this is where we are meant to be for now? Who knows what the future holds, but for the time being we are very happy campers indeed. We've never seen the Ulysses butterfly again, which does leave a stain of sadness, but in a way it is lovely to know we have not needed it.

"If there ever

comes a day

when we can't be together,

keep me in your heart,

I'll stay there

forever."

A. A. Milne

Winnie the Pooh

Gentle Whispers

Footnote: Not long after all the drama had settled down and we were enjoying our beautifully revamped home, a letter arrived in the mail. It has been such a joy to receive these words of encouragement over the years. This one was from a new friend who contacted me after reading my first book. We have become pen friends and enjoy sharing so many like-minded thoughts and hobbies. I love receiving her news and the poetry, photos and small gifts she sends. I am always on the lookout for something I can share with her too, something that might bring a smile to her day.

Well, can you guess what was in the envelope? Yes, a packet of numerous blue butterflies. Some resting on flowers, some fluttering, some close up to the petals. Oh, how my heart sang, knowing Jenny had heard a Gentle Whisper, responded, and confirmed again that I was meant to share this story. Did I ever doubt? Ummmm! I do hope it blesses you too, knowing that no matter how difficult a situation may seem, God will never leave you and will use His plans and purposes to reveal the outcome He knows is best for you.

Reflections: So often in life we are faced with experiences we would rather not have. It is only through the dark times that we can find the light. When we suffer sorrow, we can then appreciate abundant joy.

Have you ever seen a dear little child who has fallen and grazed their knee? Goodness, you would think it was the end of the world. Of course it hurts, and the blood oozing from the wound is not a pretty sight. Possibly the embarrassment is too much to bear, but then comes the hug from his mummy. The care she takes cleaning and dressing the wound, even though it stings, is just what the little one needs. The gentle voice of Mummy, the tender strokes of her hand, and then the ice block from the freezer after the ordeal is over is exactly what this brave little soldier needs.

Maybe some of you are going through traumatic times where there seems to be no way out. Life does seem utterly unfair at times, and sometimes it really is, but in these moments I hope you too can experience a Gentle Whisper with wings, or a hug from Heaven or a loved one, that will give you exactly what you need.

Catherine Grace

Life is full of ups and downs, light and darkness, right and wrong, joy and sadness. The list is endless. But in these times of fully experiencing life, we have the opportunity to learn just how strong we really are and how resilient we can be. We learn to be overcomers, but most of all we learn the purpose and fulfilment of life. And life is all about saying goodbye.

When times of farewell come, whether because of death, leaving, the end of an era, or even parting with a beloved pet, I am so grateful I don't live this life alone. I choose to put my faith in God, who is with me every step of the way. I can't imagine it any other way.

Peace will Come

The thought...
The streams of life flow out of control.
I do my best to guard my soul.
Do others see, or will I be crushed
in the riverbed that's turned to dust.

The fear...
Why must I follow this dreary season?
Won't someone explain its rhyme or reason?
For the sounds of the rain are all I hear,
with its waves of despair that are so near.

The longing...
A yearning for peace stirs in my mind.
I look up to see, but I must be blind
to the answered prayers that lie ahead.
What must I do, where will I tread?

Gentle Whispers

The hope…
I reach out toward the gentle flow…
To gain all that I've longed for–I must let go!
With hand on my heart for one more day,
peace 'will' come to show the way.

The doubt…
Yet, what if it doesn't, what will I do?
So many are suffering, my neighbours too.
I look to the sky and see only grey clouds,
yes, the rumbling of thunder clear and loud!

The healing…
I ponder the memories I've left behind,
then the beauty of kindness calms my mind.
So don't look back, that only brings strife.
As prayers are prayed, I breathe in new life.

The belief…
No matter what seasons lay ahead,
I'm grateful for my daily bread.
Through wind and rain, famine or flood,
Peace will come, my heart WILL trust.
C. G. – 2022
(My thoughts after times of hardship, drought and floods.)

Chapter Seven:
Why Are We Waiting?

"Why are we waiting,

Slowly dehydrating,

Why are we waiting,

oh why do we wait?

Why are we waiting,

We should be integrating.

Why are we waiting,

oh why are we waiting,

oh why are we waiting,

Oh why do we wait."

Anon.

Have you ever been on a bus or on a tour when a rendition of this rather silly song breaks out? Apart from breaking the boredom of waiting, usually for a toilet stop (and ohhh those ladies' queues) or for some refreshments, it does bring a smile to everyone's dial. I'm not sure who wrote this rhyme, but it seems to have come from a football club in England and also a boarding school where the pupils, getting very hungry, sang this little ditty with knives and forks in hand, banging on the table in time with the tune. I'm sure they sang with great gusto as well! With further research, it was also written by a Scottish rock band called Bis in 1999 with some added verses and a few different lines. Unfortunately though, the beautiful music score they used for their silly song is O Come All Ye Faithful! Dearie me!

Waiting certainly is a part of everyday life isn't it? We wait on the phone; we wait in queues; we wait for babies to arrive; we wait for the home bell to ring after a long day at school; we wait for a noisy neighbour to turn their loud music down; we wait to be served in a shop. Ohhh who can forget those Kmart checkout lines, especially at

Christmas time. We wait for dinner to be cooked. The list goes on and on. Some waiting can be really frustrating and even make us upset, especially if it is for a well-deserved apology that never comes, but some waiting is worth it with a beautiful outcome at the end. I try to remind myself there is a perfect time for everything as it says in the well-known verses in Ecclesiastes:

There is a time for everything,

and a season for every activity under the heavens:

a time to be born and a time to die,

a time to plant and a time to uproot,

a time to kill and a time to heal,

a time to tear down and a time to build,

a time to weep and a time to laugh,

a time to mourn and a time to dance,

a time to scatter stones and a time to gather them,

a time to embrace and a time to refrain from embracing,

a time to search and a time to give up,

a time to keep and a time to throw away,

a time to tear and a time to mend,

a time to be silent and a time to speak,

a time to love and a time to hate,

a time for war and a time for peace…

He has made everything beautiful in its time.

Ecclesiastes 3:1–8, 11 NIV

I think that just about covers everything doesn't it? How assured we can be in knowing everything has a purposeful time, especially in our times of waiting. It's having confidence that everything, not just some things, but everything, has its own designated time to come into being. What a load of worry and frustration that takes off our shoulders. Waiting can be a time of consolation if we will only remember this.

I remember reading a story once about the accomplished and talented photographer Ken Duncan. His waiting moment is beautiful and shows the wonderful experience you can have if you simply wait, no matter the conditions. Maybe this will prompt you to have a look at his beautiful and creative style of photography on his webpage. The story is there for all to see along with his God-given gift. This particular photo was a mountain-top scene of wildflowers where many photographers were waiting for the special moment. I remember Ken saying he left because the light wasn't good, but he returned later in the day. Then the rain and a huge storm set in, but he waited it out and was rewarded with the most beautiful sight of light and colours in a brilliant rainbow.

Photographers have to be so patient. Two of my family members are very gifted professional photographers. One is a graphic designer, multimedia presenter and photographer, and the other is a baby and family photographer and events coordinator. Sooo much waiting and more! Can you imagine waiting for little ones to co-operate, or the adults trying to get their little ones to stay still and smile? The finished product is always awe-inspiring and definitely worth the wait.

A prayer I often pray, especially for my family who work so hard to make ends meet, comes from the Bible. Their jobs are all very demanding and I am so proud of the amount of time they put into their careers while also running their households and families. The verses aren't really a prayer, but I love to make Bible verses into prayers. I find the words are often just what I'm looking for, and it isn't unusual for childhood Sunday school verses to come to mind in those Gentle Whispers. We would recite many scriptures by heart. I'm so grateful I was brought up in church, even with the shortcomings and very strict religious rules I have had to overcome over the years. Churches aren't perfect and have a long way to go before they stop offending many in the community, but when songs and verses come to mind in beautiful Gentle Whispers, I know without a doubt God is watching and knows exactly what I need at any given moment. These verses from Isaiah make the most beautiful prayer:

Gentle Whispers

"But those who wait on the Lord

shall renew their strength;

They shall mount up with wings like eagles,

they shall run and not be weary,

they shall walk and not faint."

Isaiah 40:31 NKJV

So with this verse and others that suit the time, I will put the person's name in and ask and thank the Lord for His answered prayer. I then believe the strength will come so they won't be weary and will not faint, and will be able to successfully complete the tasks at hand.

It is such a beautiful thing to do, to wait on the Lord. I guess what it really means is to put time aside to spend with God. If you don't know Him or believe in Him, it may sound a little strange that someone would want to spend time with an invisible being. Many people who need peace and solace in their everyday lives find yoga or meditation helpful. I'm sure it is. Anything that helps slow our racing minds in this stressful world must be helpful. You can combine yoga and meditation with your faith beliefs too, but I find the person of Jesus, who is so very real to me, the only one I want to draw aside with. It is during these quiet times we often hear the Gentle Whispers. If we are constantly buzzing around and not taking the time to listen and wait for the answers we desperately need, we will never hear and our lives will become exhausting.

Answers don't always come when we want them to either, but in the drawing aside, in whatever way you choose, the waiting becomes bearable and easier to live with. I highly recommend you take heed of the following words from a poem I wrote many years ago when I was praying for a friend who was waiting for a very important answer. She just couldn't stop. Her life was so stressful and her days filled with anxiety. I hope this Gentle Whisper, which came in the form of a poem, helped her and can also help you while you are waiting for whatever it is you long to know.

Catherine Grace

Draw Aside

Draw aside and rest awhile,
Come find a quiet place
to rest your soul,
restore your thoughts
and calm the racing pace.

Draw aside and rest awhile,
There's beauty all around.
The bird in flight,
the flower in bloom,
can you hear my sound?

Draw aside and rest awhile
I've made all this for you.
Breathe in the fragrance
of my creation,
it's here I'll meet with you.

C. G. '98.

I do hope you can find a quiet place, an oasis or secluded setting that is your very own, where you can welcome the tranquil surroundings and hear the Gentle Whispers. If you don't have such a place, what a wonderful thing to do! Off you go, it's time to find one. That sounds exciting!

This next true story brings to light the waiting moments when we can be there for someone else. I had never thought having a therapy dog would lead me into a situation like this, but I'm so very grateful and blessed it did.

Gentle Whispers

A Heavenly Appointment

Our little Bichon Frise, Maggie, who had been a therapy dog for about five years, was asked if she would be able to sit with an elderly lady whose time was drawing to an end before she was to go to her Heavenly home. Maggie had visited this dear soul many times over the five years I had been taking her to this aged-care home. The lady who had requested Maggie found that having a soft, fluffy doggie lying next to her brought so much calm and peace. Maggie certainly was a gentle and very placid dog who didn't mind at all being snuggled up next to someone, especially when they stroked her soft white curly fur and gently whispered sweet words to her. With this lady being in palliative care, we knew it wouldn't be too long before the phone would ring and Maggie would be on her way to this very important mission. What an honour!

The wait was actually more difficult than I had first anticipated. It meant I couldn't be too far from home, and Maggie had to be groomed and ready to go each day. She certainly had to look and feel her very best for this most important occasion. I also didn't know if the call would come during the day or the night. Of course, I was quite okay with either. It was also tinged with a great deal of sadness because when the call did come, it meant this lady was near the end of her life. So for the next couple of weeks, each day when I arose I was waiting, and then each night before I went to bed, I was waiting, and waiting throughout the sleepless nights wondering if this would be the time. Thankfully Maggie had no idea, as nothing really changed for her except for a little extra pampering each day, and she was already used to visiting this facility each week.

Then, late one afternoon, the call did come. I prayed it would be just as this angel, who was waiting for her wings, needed, and it was. I placed Maggie next to the dear soul in her favourite spot, tucked in close to her thigh and under her arm so she could pat and stroke as much as she needed. We are so fortunate, aren't we, that modern medicines can make this time pain-free and comfortable for the patient.

A Gentle Whisper came in the form of a thought that I should step outside and give the family privacy at this very sad and memorable time. With all the previous visits over the years, I had always stayed with Maggie to chat to the patients and make sure they were feeling comfortable with her. I had no idea what would happen if I walked away out of sight, then I remembered part of Maggie's training with the company she worked for. One of the trainers would hold on to your dog, and then you were to walk away slowly and be just out of sight. This was to see if the dog panicked or became distressed. Maggie never did and always passed these training days with flying colours. It really was her destiny to be a therapy dog.

I quietly slipped away just outside the door and it was only a few moments until the daughter came and asked me to collect Maggie, as she had done her job well. Dear little pet. I was so proud of her. She hadn't moved and only raised her head when she saw me come back into the room. I gave my condolences to the family and quickly removed Maggie, and we were on our way back to the car where I cried my eyes out! How wonderful it is that these precious pets seem to know just what we humans need at any given time. It is also a comfort to know the animal kingdom and all of nature hear from their Creator too. It isn't man who tells the sun to rise, the seasons to begin and end, or the precious pets to show us the love and companionship we need. I don't believe it is by chance either! Being reminded of Jesus saying "my sheep hear my voice", the animals knowing they were to enter the ark two by two, and a dove searching for the olive leaf to prove there was dry land, weren't whims or accidents, but responses to a Gentle Whisper from their Creator's command. There is a Proverb that also commands us to be merciful and kind to the animals. In Psalm 150:6 it says:

"Let everything that has breath,

Praise the Lord

Praise ye the Lord!" NIV

Have you ever seen a cormorant spread its shimmery black wings? You just thought they were drying their wings didn't you? Well, maybe they are, but would I be going too far in thinking they may also be praising the Lord their Creator while they wait? It is also said birds fulfil this concept by doing what they are designed to do: warble, tweet, and chirp in the most glorious birdsong to bring praise to the Lord.

Wild animals and all cattle,

small creatures and flying birds,

Kings of the earth and all nations,

you princes and all rulers on earth,

young men and women,

old men and children.

let them praise the name of the Lord,

for His name alone is exalted;

His splendour is above the earth

and the Heavens.

Psalm 148:10–13 NIV

When the Psalmist wrote this verse, it is interesting to note he saw the importance of everyone bringing praise to the Lord. There was no one left out, and everyone was equal in their praises to God. It is also written in the Word that people have dominion over the plants and the animals. What a responsibility! Not only in looking after our planet, but also in treating kindly all the animals that are put in our care. When we think of them as creatures that bring praise to God, as the above verse says, surely it shows us the importance of giving them the best care we are able to.

There are many true stories of animals saving human lives that really touch the heart and confirm the fact that they do have a knowing, as if they are being instructed by a higher being. One such story is one I was told by an entertaining patient I met at the same centre where Maggie comforted the lady in her last moments.

Stefan's Story:

Every week Stefan would wait patiently for Maggie's visits. From the time we arrived at the retirement centre, staff would let us know as we walked by, saying, "Stefan's waiting," or "Stefan has been ready and waiting for over an hour!" It always looked as if he had taken special care with his attire on visiting day and his hair was always slicked back, looking very dapper indeed! Now don't get too carried away with your thoughts here. All this fuss wasn't made for me but for his favourite girl, Maggie! I can assure you the feeling was also mutual, as Maggie would lead me to his door with her little unique skip and wagging tail in great excitement.

Stefan was a strong Polish man with hands so large you could be forgiven for hoping you never got in the way of them, but that would never happen as Stefan was the gentlest of souls. He would pick Maggie up with one hand and place her on his bed, and then the fun would begin with patting, tumbling, and hiding under the blankets. It was always the same routine, and when both man and dog were a little puffed, these familiar words would come:

"Have I told you the story of a dog from my village where I grew up in Poland?"

Both Maggie and I would give Stefan our full attention, letting him think it was the first time we had heard this true story. I would get comfy in the armchair and Maggie would remain on the bed with Stefan's big hands covering her soft curly coat with his soothing pats.

"Well, this dog was a hero! One day a young brother took his little sister, who was very small, for a walk to the channel. The little girl must have fallen in, as the brother arrived home without her. Many people from the village searched and searched but she could not be found. Night-time came and everyone was so worried, especially her parents who wondered if they would ever see their little girl again. The next morning all the village people went out again looking everywhere, but the poor little girl could not be found."

Maggie and I sat with bated breath while Stefan took a breath, and Maggie wasn't worried at all how long it took to get to the end. His large masculine hands covered her whole head with gentle strokes. Stefan collected his thoughts and continued:

Gentle Whispers

"Well, this went on for two whole days. Everyone in the village was so upset and we could only imagine how the brother was feeling. On the evening of the second day, a man who lived near the channel decided to go and fetch his dog to see if it could help in the search. When the owner thought about it, the dog had been very quiet for two days since the little girl disappeared and had only come for his food. He went out the back to the dog kennel and had to peer right inside to see the dog curled up toward the back. When he called the dog, it didn't move but tried to go further into the kennel to show the owner it may have been guarding something."

Stefan's voice grew louder with great excitement as he revealed the end of his story:

"So what do you think that man found in the back of his dog's kennel? It was the little girl, safe and sound asleep. The dog must have dragged her up from the water's edge and kept her warm in his kennel for two whole days. Everyone was so excited and relieved and the dog was treated like a real hero. The village people would often be seen throwing a bone over the fence or giving him a pat, telling him what a brave, clever dog he was."

I'm so glad Stefan had the opportunity to share his story with Maggie and me each week. It seemed to bring so much pleasure to this dear man, remembering an event from his younger years in his native land, and we always agreed there is no finer friend than a furry canine one. What a blessing it was to know Maggie was patiently waited for each week and could bring so much love and fun to this gentleman's day.

Reflections: I certainly do not want to take away the fact of just how difficult some waiting times can be. We have just walked beside a dear friend who has been waiting for test results which really could have gone either way. The physical pain was excruciating, but so was the mental and heartfelt pain during the time of waiting. For some reason the wait went on for about four weeks and we admired the faith this courageous lady demonstrated.

Catherine Grace

Faith is not having
all of the answers
all of the time.
It is still believing
during the waiting.

C. G. '24

When the waiting time was finally over, the results were a huge relief. We were all so grateful to God for His answered prayers.

Distractions can be a marvellous way of spending your days while you wait. This is when you can ask for Gentle Whispers to while away the hours. Maybe there is a friend you haven't caught up with for some time. Nothing is finer than a lovely cuppa at a favourite café to share some love and care. Walks along the beach or through the woods can certainly help ease your mind as you experience all the beauty around you. Nature certainly is a precious gift for times like this. It is often in these places Gentle Whispers from above can come and quieten your heart and ease your worries. These moments can also bring a skip to your step and a smile to your dial.

Gazing at beauty is such a refreshing, healing and wonderful provision. Why not take a trip to your local gallery? There certainly is brilliant artwork there, where your thoughts will be distracted by the talents of these very skilful artists whose work will take your breath away at just how they accomplished such fine masterpieces. A trip to the movies or turning on Netflix is another way to take your mind off things. Comedies can be a real distraction at these times, as laughter really is the best medicine. For some, reading is another form of distraction that can help you through some waiting hours. It isn't unusual to see people reading on a train waiting for their destination or reading a magazine or book whilst waiting at the doctor's surgery. I'm sure you can think of a whole host of distractions too, so while you wait for whatever it is, I do hope the end result is just the good news you need. You also might be amazed at the God Whisper that can come during these times.

Gentle Whispers

Recently I was waiting on the Lord for an answer to a situation I was in that I had no idea how to get out of, or how to move on from. It seemed to me this dilemma was not of my own doing, but something very hurtful and sadly inflicted on me. Yes, even little old ladies with greying hair can have such moments, and yes, we do still have feelings that can come unstuck and cause such sadness at times — sob, sniffle, tissues please!

It was very late at night, as I am a night owl anyway, but I knew if I went to bed to try and find sleep, it would not come, so I turned on the television to a favourite programme I knew was on. It is one that always brings comfort to my soul as I watch the beautiful English countryside scenes and quaint cottages on view. The sound was down low and I was praying quietly in my mind, waiting for some answers and resolutions to my problem. Nothing seemed to be coming, so I raised my hands to Heaven and prayed out loud, "Here I am Lord, please take this from me, for what else can I do?"

In that very moment a voice from the television show came on very clearly and loudly: "You will just have to trust me with that!" I promise you I had not touched the remote to increase the sound, nor had I expected such a quick response. Even though it wasn't a solution to the actual problem, it was the answer I needed. Sometimes circumstances in our lives are too big and difficult for us to try and work out. Often we make the situations worse by trying, as I have done many times with good intentions! I'm not sure why the host of the programme was telling the people she was showing the house to that they would have to trust her. I had missed what was said previously while I was praying, but those words were exactly what I needed. Of course, the sceptics out there will say it was just a coincidence, but as I've already explained previously, there are no coincidences in my life, but there are plans, purposes and Gentle Whispers.

Another favourite waiting implement for me is music. Oh how I love those sweet melodies and harmonies that send peaceful sound waves through my mind. Music can calm the mind in an instant and bring peace just when we need it. One of my favourite music styles is Irish or Celtic music. For some reason the minor tones make me feel all warm and fuzzy — just what I need in a waiting moment. I do believe music can touch the soul where medicines can't.

A famous musician once said:

>*"I play the notes*
>
>*as they are written,*
>
>*but it is God*
>
>*who makes the music."*
>
>*Johann Sebastian Bach.*

Some of the old hymns have such beautiful tunes with words that go right to the heart. One hymn written after a devastating time of waiting was penned when the writer's four daughters died in the sinking of the S. S. Ville *du Havre*. Horatio Spafford had been delayed from travelling to England from Chicago, so he sent his four daughters and his wife ahead of him. During the crossing of the Atlantic Ocean, the ship sank rapidly after a collision with another vessel, the *Loch Earn*. All four of Spafford's daughters died. His wife, Anna, survived and sent him the now-famous telegram, "Saved alone." Shortly afterwards, as Spafford travelled to meet his grieving wife, he was inspired to write these words as his ship passed near where his daughters had perished in the depths of the sea. A composer, Philip Bliss, later named the tune *Ville du Havre*, after the stricken vessel (Ref. Wikipedia.org). The mellow tones of this hymn are so soothing and beautiful. I wonder how many people over the years have been deeply touched by its notes and words.

It Is Well With My Soul

When peace like a river

attendeth my way,

When sorrows like sea billows roll;

Whatever my lot, Thou hast taught me to know,

It is well, it is well with my soul.

Gentle Whispers

It is well (it is well)

With my soul (with my soul)

It is well, it is well with my soul.

Horatio Spafford, 20 Oct. 1828 – 16 Oct. 1888.

There are five other verses to this beautiful hymn, which I encourage you to read and listen to at your leisure. There are many facets of waiting in this story. I'm sure Horatio would have been waiting for news that his dear family had arrived safely in England, but sadly this wasn't to be. Then came the long wait for news after the sinking of the ship that took his girls' lives, and that news arrived in the form of a brief telegram from his grieving wife. Life wasn't as quick or instant as it is today with our mobile phones and the internet, so the waiting would have been incredibly worrisome.

After such a traumatic and heartbreaking event, I'm encouraged by the hymn above, which I'm sure came as a Gentle Whisper from Horatio's Heavenly Father as he passed the very place where the ship went down. What faith, and what a beautiful gift has been given to the world through Horatio Spafford in sharing his deeply felt song with us all. It's impossible to count how many times these words have brought encouragement and peace to people in their moments of need, especially in their waiting.

I'll never forget the time my youngest son sang and played this hymn during our morning service at church. It came at a time when the words were needed so much, and his rendition touched many. I'm so grateful he was listening to those Gentle Whispers that morning, as it was a spur-of-the-moment decision to sing the hymn that day. How beautiful it is when Gentle Whispers are acted on so spontaneously.

Maybe it isn't the older hymns you enjoy most. I also appreciate more modern music, especially faith-based ones. We are all uniquely made, and our individual tastes make the world a better place. For some reason, being a girl from the country has not given me a love of country music, much to my husband's dismay. He loves it, especially the bluegrass style. I shudder at the thought, but I'm happy to move to another room or go for a walk when he feels the need for a little 'yee-ha'!

It was when a lovely friend of mine was waiting for news from New Zealand about whether her mum was still with us that this song came to me in a Gentle Whisper while I was praying for her. I was able to find the song and sent it to her. She had heard it before, but the reminder brought her hope and comfort at a very sad time. Maybe it is just what you need to hear today, whatever it is you are waiting for.

Take Courage

Slow down, take time

'Breathe in,' He said

He'd reveal what's to come

The thoughts in His mind

Always higher than mine

He'll reveal all to come

Take courage my heart

Stay steadfast my soul

He's in the waiting

He's in the waiting

hold onto your hope

As your triumph unfolds

He's never failing

He's never failing

Sing praise my soul

Find strength in joy

Let His words lead you on

Do not forget

Gentle Whispers

His great faithfulness
He'll finish all He's begun.

And you hold the stars
Who call them each by name
Will surely keep your promise to me
That I will rise in your victory
So take courage my heart
Stay steadfast my soul
He's in the waiting
He's in the waiting
He's in the waiting
Waiting.

Bethel Music – DiMarco, Jeremy Riddle, Joel Taylor.
Produced by Ran Jackson and Chris Greely.

Will you take the time to listen for those Gentle Whispers in your waiting time? They are there and they will come as the many promises in His Word tell us so. You are never alone.

Gentle Whispers

... a comfy glow of His Love?

Chapter Eight: Can You Hear Me?

"Someone told me:

Only those who care about you,

can hear you

when you are quiet."

Anon.

Hearing and listening would have to be the most complicated and potentially difficult, yet also helpful and encouraging, senses of the human body. It is through this instrument of our body that most of our communication and decision-making is made. It is also from this part of our anatomy that most of our emotions and feelings are reached, e.g. if I hear beautiful sounds, I feel at peace; if I hear pleasant words, I feel all warm and fuzzy; if I hear yelling and screaming, I feel frightened or alarmed. I read this quote not long ago, so I looked it up to clarify its meaning, and it really does say it all:

You seldom listen to me,

and when you do you don't hear

and when you do hear you hear wrong,

and even when you hear right

you change it so fast

that it's never the same.

Marjorie Kellogg 17.7.1922 – 19.12.2005

(Playwright, fantasy author and social worker)

So many of our misunderstandings in our relationships occur because we aren't listening intently, or we don't want to hear what is being said. Have you ever thought, 'Why do we have two ears yet only one mouth?' Well, it's a very simple answer. 'So that we can listen twice as much as we speak.' Ohhh, what a difference it would make in our world if we could only achieve that! Of course, hearing and listening are two entirely different things, yet they are so intricately connected.

Hearing: The process, function or power of perceiving sound, specifically: the special sense by which noises and tones are perceived as stimuli. (Merriam-Webster)

Listening: To pay attention to sound; to hear something with thoughtful attention; give consideration. (Merriam-Webster)

I like the above definitions of these two senses as, straight away, they point out the main difference between them both. Hearing is recognising a sound, and listening is paying attention to and trying to understand and interpret the sound. I'm sure you have come across many comical conversations where this has happened, and for some reason, the 'all-knowing ones' seem to think it is the men who have the biggest problem hearing and interpreting what is said. I certainly do not want to get into a debate, but this little quote did make me smile!

Did you know women

use about 30,000 words a day

while men use only 15,000.

Yes, because we have to repeat

everything we say!

A funny, even if rather frustrating, occurrence happened a few years ago between my hubby and me. I'm sure he won't mind me sharing it. After many months of my dear man not being able to hear me speak and many moments of actually being heard incorrectly (no, I didn't ask you to stop coughing; I said: "Do you want a coffee?!), he eventually took himself off to the audiologist for a hearing test. I had been requesting this for quite some time after many moments of waiting on the wrong corner at the wrong time; in front of the wrong shop; being stood up for a coffee date, oh, the list was endless. But of course, *I* was in those right places; someone else had heard me differently! I'm sure some of you have a knowing smile at this scenario!

Catherine Grace

It wasn't long until the brand spanking new hearing aids had arrived and were being tested out. I was quite proud of my hubby for persevering with them, as they do take some getting used to with not only the 'hearing' side of things but also with how they feel in one's ears. Everything seemed to be going so well for him, but not so well for me, as I still had to repeat everything I said. I was now convinced it had been selective hearing this whole time, and I was not one bit impressed, to say the least!

An appointment had to be made to tweak any little issues that may have arisen with the new hearing aids, so I promptly told hubby I was coming with him to see what the cure was for 'selective hearing!' As I was relaying my story of the hearing aid saga, a big broad smile appeared on the face of the audiology technician. He promptly asked me to speak into a microphone that was connected to his computer, and wouldn't you know it? My rather soft, monotone voice was the very tone hubby found the most difficult to hear. So, after a few tweaks later, life is all rosy again with conversations flowing much more freely between us. I can even speak 'sweet little nothings' and he hears me straight away!

So often we miss much of what our Heavenly Father is saying to us because we can't hear or recognise His Gentle Whispers, or don't even want to. I wonder how often He is looking down, knowing what is best for us, but thinking: "Oh, if only they would hear and listen!" It is interesting to note that the word *hear* appears 516 times in the Bible from 49 books, so we can say without a doubt that hearing is very important. In comparison, the word *listen* appears 265 times, so it is quite safe to say that, even though we all have the ability to hear what is being said, it is our free will to choose whether to listen or not.

I guess it is like living close to a railway line. When you first move into the home near those rumbling trains passing by every day, the noise would be quite annoying from hearing the rattling of the carriages as they clickety-clack past. After a few months though, it's quite remarkable that you don't even notice one just went by, and you didn't even hear it. How does the brain do that, I 'hear' you ask? Well, it is quite complicated and way out of my area of expertise, but Google does say neuroscientists have now identified a brain circuit that helps us to do just that. The circuit they identified, which is controlled by the prefrontal cortex, filters out unwanted background noise and other distracting sensory stimuli. So the fact remains: we may all be able to hear those Gentle Whispers from Heaven above, but not everyone will be listening.

This next little story tells of when I was so relieved I heard and was able to help a troubled young man who so dearly needed someone to be listening. It was quite a few years ago, so these Gentle Whispers and I have been sharing life for some time now, even though I probably wasn't aware of their importance or the full extent they could be used for. As with most things, awareness and wisdom can be actively developed. It's through life experiences, reflection and learning that this awareness comes especially as we grow in age.

In the still of the night

Night sounds are one of the most beautiful noises to hear. Have you ever noticed that as the sun is setting, birds become very vocal with their melodic birdsong? I wonder if it is Muma and Papa birds calling their young ones in for the evening, or maybe even singing grace as they tuck into their evening meal. I know this is a tad silly, but imagining such things is quite entertaining when you love nature as much as I do.

Many years ago a favourite TV show was *The Walton's*, and every night as the family were switching off their lights they would call to each other: "Goodnight Muma; goodnight Daddy; goodnight Mary-Ellen; goodnight Elizabeth; goodnight Jim Bob; and an emphasised, goodnight John-Boy!" Everyone in the family would then reply with their goodnights, with one member never answering. Yes, Jim Bob had fallen asleep. John-Boy was usually the last to reply to them all, I guess because he was the oldest son and brother, and it was the sound of his voice that would stay in everyone's memory until the next episode. John-Boy was the most popular member of the family, so the ratings proved. He was my favourite, as the actor's name was the same as my dearly departed grandfather.

One of my most favourite times to walk is night-time. Everything is so peaceful, with the dark sky filled with glistening stars, planets and the moon to keep you company. For me, it is like God is covering us all in a comfy glow of His love. A favourite verse I always take with me is Psalm 91:11–12.

> *For He will command his angels*
>
> *concerning you,*
>
> *to guard you in all your ways:*
>
> *They will lift you up in their hands,*
>
> *so that you will not strike your foot*
>
> *Against a stone. – NIV*

Isn't it a beautiful promise? Knowing we all have angels guarding and guiding us along life's journey brings so much assurance, security and comfort to our day. One very wise evangelist and teacher even wrote a book about angels. I think these quotes say it all:

"We are not alone in this world! Angels are Real! They are sent by God to protect and Help His people! Their powers are beyond human imagination!"

"We face dangers every day of which we are not even aware. Often God intervenes on our behalf through the use of His angels."

"Just as millions of angels participated in the dazzling show when the morning stars sang together at creation, so will the innumerable host of angels help bring to pass God's prophetic declaration throughout the time and into eternity."

Angels: God's Secret Agents by Billy Graham 7.11.1918 – 21.2.2018

What a wonderful blessing it is to know we can go about our daily tasks knowing the Creator of the universe will send His angels to protect and help us. I know angels aren't omniscient, nor are they omnipresent. They are there, waiting for their Creator to give instructions at any given moment. We are also warned never to put Satan on par with God, because actually he is a fallen angel, roaming around waiting for someone to devour (1 Peter 5:8–10). Yes, we must be on guard, not giving him any reason to be in our lives.

Gentle Whispers

This does conjure up all sorts of questions and confusion about the troubles in the world today. Where are those angels then, when we need them? Why isn't God protecting us like the Bible says? Why is the evil angel allowed to cause so much destruction? Apart from the fact that this detour is taking me way off course from those Gentle Whispers... or is it? Maybe you are hearing one right now. I will say though, I trust in God's perfect plan.

How many in the world today are trusting God; following Jesus; believing in His angels guiding and protecting us; living a life in accordance with eternal life and the heavenly realm? It is about a third. Does that explain it? I know some of these thoughts hit hard, but I do believe they are worth saying. We all need a shake-up sometimes, and I am no theologian, but another quote from Billy Graham's daughter is oh so true:

"For years we've been telling God to get out of our schools, to get out of our government and to get out of our lives. And being the gentleman He is, I believe He has calmly backed out. How can we expect God to give us His blessings and His protection if we demand He leave us alone!"

Anne Graham (in an interview with Bryant Gumbel)

I hope this little interlude has encouraged you to thank God every day for the protection and help from His angels, just as I do along my peaceful night walks. I also hope you will be bold and care enough to tell your stories. Our dark and sick world needs them.

On this particular evening, it was looking like I was going to walk alone. I was just about to change my mind but felt a prompting that I was still to go; yes, this Gentle Whisper was definitely a prompting. The cold, crisp air was setting in for the night, but that never bothered me, even in the high tablelands where we lived. The twinkling of the stars always seemed to shine brighter in this area of the country, especially when we turned the corner and ventured out of town along a road with no street lights. I quickened my steps to where there was a railway crossing hoping I hadn't missed the famous Indian Pacific that would rattle its way along on its way to Perth. It was always fun to see it travelling by with all the passengers aboard on their three-night holiday across our wide and unique land. What diverse and strange scenery they would see along the way. Through cities; farmland; forests; deserted county towns; the Australian bush; the red dirt deserts and the yellow sandy plains which make up our fascinating country are so popular to see from this train.

As I was crossing the line, I heard a familiar voice catching up behind me. My eldest son had decided he needed a break from his studies, so I was grateful for the company. In a busy family, time alone with one child at a time was rare, and with this one being the quietest of my three, I was happy to catch up on his views of his world, and the world at large.

The moon was shining so brightly this particular night that we rarely needed to put our torches on. The familiar sounds when passing different paddocks showed us we were right on course too. One of the property's dams was very close to the fence line, and I loved hearing the different croaky voices of the frogs that lived there. I would imagine the largest frog being the choir master and bringing all the other frogs in when it was their time to harmonise and join the chorus. It really was a joy to hear the calls of nature at night.

Owls and tawny frogmouth bird calls were fascinating to hear at night too. One property had an abundance of trees creating woodland at the front of their acreage, where we would often hear the different 'woo-hoo' or 'hoot-hoot' calls. The tawny frogmouth has a different call altogether being a low-pitched, repetitive sequence of 'ooom-ooom-ooom-ooom' sounds (well, that is how Google describes it, she says with a giggle!). Apparently, these calls are made so the partners of these magnificent birds can hear their way home when they are night-hunting for supper.

Another reason I love the night sounds is because they assure us we are not alone. God in His generosity has made such a diverse playground of creatures for us to enjoy during the day and the night. It would be such a shame to miss the night variety because we were afraid of the dark or didn't feel comfortable venturing out when the sun disappeared behind the horizon. It is during these tranquil night moments we can often hear those Gentle Whispers a little more clearly.

We walked on, sometimes chatting and sometimes in silence, waiting to identify the next creature sound waiting to entertain us. Well, it was actually me who was being more entertained. I think my son was just being very long-suffering and humouring Mother! Before long, we were entering back into town where the misty streetlight glow of the city was waiting to greet us with the knowledge that home was not too far away. Then we heard it, a very different sound, a human sound calling to us as we passed by.

We stopped and turned around to be greeted by a young man who had taken shelter on the steps of a local corner shop. He seemed very afraid and unsure of his bearings. He looked to be only in his late teens or early twenties. After a short conversation, we realised he had been discharged from a local mental health facility on the other side of town. The poor fellow had no family around and was told he could go to a church where they had been notified of his release and would be able to look after him until he could return to his family and home.

Sadly, when he arrived at the church, which happened to be the church we attended, it was all shut with no one around at all. There had obviously been crossed lines in communication. We offered to take him home with us, which wasn't something I would normally do, but we couldn't leave this young man stranded on the steps in the dark when it was going to be such a cold night and he was already showing signs of anxiousness and stress. I was so grateful my eldest son was with me at the time… not for my own protection, but for the young man to feel a little more comfortable coming home with us.

When we arrived home, we gave the lad something warm to drink and rang the Pastor of the church, who we found out had been waiting for this boy to arrive. But when he hadn't, the thought was that he must have made other arrangements, so the Pastor had left to make enquiries with the people who had discharged him. The Pastor soon arrived to take care of the young man and, as the story unfolded, we realised the boy had become lost on his way to the church, arriving much later than the designated time.

Catherine Grace

I guess the moral of this rather simple story and most of the others, actually is, we not only are to be listening for the Gentle Whispers but to act on them. Goodness knows what would have happened if I hadn't rethought going for the walk that night, and also the fact that my son had decided to catch up after me. There really is something quite confirming about *being in the right place at the right time!*

> *"It's not enough to be in the right place*
>
> *at the right time.*
>
> *You have to be the right person*
>
> *in the right place,*
>
> *at the right time."*
>
> T. Harv Eker – 10.6.54
>
> *Author/motivational speaker.*

A similar situation happened near where we live just last month. It had been a very sad day… the day we had to say goodbye to our beautiful little Bichon Frise, Maggie. She lived to 15 years of age and had been such a faithful and loyal companion all those years. Her health deteriorated quickly, but the illness was not treatable and an operation was out of the question at her age, with no guarantee of a quality of life afterwards. The operation would have had to be long and extensive, which she may not even have come through.

To make the day even sadder, Hubby was away, and waiting for him to be home would have meant more suffering for our little pooch. The decision was made, but it really was the most difficult thing to have to do. I had sat up with Maggie every night that week hoping and praying she would just fall asleep and not wake up, so the decision wouldn't be ours to make. Who would ever want to make that call? To end the life of a beautiful living thing that had been the most precious gift, not only to us but to many others who knew her, was just too overwhelming! Sadly though, it wasn't to be, and on the last visit to the veterinary clinic, I asked the vet if she should have any more tests to confirm her situation, and a very loud and clear "no" came back. Phone calls were made to Hubby and, with him on speaker phone, she was put to sleep.

Gentle Whispers

As you can imagine, I was devastated and really didn't want to go home to our empty house, so I visited favourite places that afternoon where we would often take Maggie for her walks. We are blessed to live near many beaches and lakes, and the beautiful scenery really did quieten my heart, but I still had to go home. Caring family and friends had offered to be with me, but I knew I would be better left to my own thoughts, as upsetting others would have also been more upsetting for me. Evening was setting in so I decided it was time. I headed home, put the car in the garage and then collected the mail.

Once I had the mail, I turned around to head inside, but then decided, "No, I'll just turn back around and head down to the pond," which was in a beautiful recreational area, "to see if the frog choir was practising that night." As I turned the last corner down to the pond, I could see a car parked in a very unusual place with its parking lights still on, so I went to investigate. As I drew closer, I could see a shadow of someone standing at the driver's door and a little "Hello, is someone there?" wafted to my ears. What unfolded in the next moments was quite remarkable, which made me realise again that Gentle Whispers had prompted my heart to change course and not go directly home. It was definitely another 'being in the right place at the right time' moment.

The driver of the car had only moved into the area the week before and had become disoriented in the dark, trying to remember where her garage was. When she found it, driving her car into the garage was another matter, as she was having to steer in the opposite direction from what she was used to in her previous garage. So she decided to just park it on the grass and was praying someone would come along to rescue her and lo and behold, it was me! Another sad part of the tale is that she had also had a fall trying to carry her shopping into her little cottage, so everything was left on the grass and there she was, believing someone would come along who could drive her car into the garage for her and help carry her shopping into her new home.

Don't you just love her faith and patience? I have been inspired by this lady since meeting her. We have become friends and our chats together have shown not only likeminded beliefs but also common people in our lives. To say it is a small world is an understatement! It has been truly amazing. In one conversation it was realised this lady's best friend had been my Sunday school teacher fifty years ago, and she is also known to other members of my family! I asked her on one of my visits what she would have done if I hadn't come along. Very firmly, and without having to even contemplate her reply, she said, "Oh, I knew God was not going to leave me standing there all night, so I knew *you* would come!"

"No friendship is an accident."

— *O. Henry – writer of Heart of the West (2015)*

As I left her home in the still of the night, I stopped by the pond and, for some reason, the frog choir was singing its most melodic song. Ohhh, those harmonies! I knew without a doubt I could face going home to our empty house with no excited doggie to greet me, because I wasn't really alone, was I? The experience I had just been through was enough reassurance and just what I needed to give me strength to face whatever was ahead. The comfort from my Heavenly Father, who was there for this stranded lady that night, was also there for me. What a privilege it was that I could be of help to someone else, which in turn helped me when I was so sad. I'm so grateful He chose me to be His messenger on that dark and dismal night!

Reflections: One of the most beautiful realisations about Gentle Whispers is that I mostly find they are a prompting to be in the right place at the right time and if it is you receiving the prompting, then you are certainly the right person. You are definitely fully qualified for whatever the task may be. It's often when we overthink things that we start to doubt whether we heard right: was it really a thought from above or just my own? Could I possibly do what is being suggested? Well, something I have learnt over the years is to just step out and do it. The more we ponder or procrastinate, the harder we make it for ourselves, not to forget the blessings we will miss out on, for others and also for ourselves. God is never going to ask you to do something you aren't capable of doing, and He is certainly not going to ask you to do something that isn't loving, caring and kind.

Gentle Whispers

I love this quote from a famous author who in his day was known to be quite controversial in writing about the poor and needy:

"No one is useless in this world

who lightens the

burdens of another."

— Charles Dickens (7.2.1812 – 9.6.1870)

I might add too, it is often when we reach out to help others when we are in need of a little love and understanding ourselves, that we receive the greater blessings. It really is wonderful to be living in the eternal realm of plans and purposes that are being revealed every day as we walk along this journey of life. I hope you believe this too. What a sad state of affairs it would be to miss all the amazing 'God surprises' He has waiting for us each day. Oh, if only the world would realise this and put their trust in Him and start living to serve others and to act on those Gentle Whispers.

Do you ever let your thoughts go to the hereafter and wonder what is on the 'other side'? I often do, as my faith believes our life here on earth really is only the beginning. Eternal life is something I really look forward to, and I do wonder at times why it is taking so long for the 'end times' to be made known. But trust I must, and I do know that one day all will be revealed. One thing that does have me often wondering is what will be waiting for me when I do arrive. Will St Peter really be at the Pearly Gates? Will my parents and other family members know I have arrived? Will my doggies be bounding over the Rainbow Bridge (the place some people believe God has for all our beloved pets) to greet me?

There are many Bible verses about creatures in Heaven. Even Billy Graham was once noted as saying:

"God will have prepared everything

for our perfect happiness.

If it takes my dog being there in Heaven,

he'll be there!"

Catherine Grace

Thank you, Billy Graham, I am hanging onto that thought!

One thing I do hope I don't find there waiting for me though is a huge pile with my name on it saying, "Cathy's missed moments!" I know God's amazing grace will cover it all and, of course, if I did miss a moment, then I know He would have graciously given it to someone else who was listening at the time. How wonderful it is, though, to be living 'in the moment' every day, waiting for those Gentle Whispers and looking out for where we can be of help to others. It is a spiritual truth that says, "He who has an ear, let him hear!" It happens to be one of Jesus's favourite expressions and is a line used in many of His parables and in the letters in Revelation. It really is why we are here: to show a little love and kindness to those who cross our path and those who God knows need a little help through some heavenly intervention.

Oh, this song has just popped into my mind. It does capture it all. I'll be showing my age again by sharing it, but I guess by now you've already worked out I am an oldish girl! I'm planning on the 'ish' part staying with me for quite a while yet. They do say old is only how you feel, well some days I wonder why I'm still here, but on others I feel like a teenager! Sing along with me if you know it!

Try a little Kindness

Sung by

Glen Campbell 1969

If you see your brother standing by the road

with a heavy load from the seeds he sowed.

And if you see your sister falling by the way,

just stop and say "you're going the wrong way.

You've got to try a little kindness,

yes show a little kindness.

just shine your light for everyone to see,

and if you try a little kindness,

Gentle Whispers

then you'll overlook the blindness

of narrow-minded people

on the narrow-minded streets.

Don't walk around the down and out,

lend a helping hand instead of doubt

and the kindness that you show everyday

will help someone along their way.

You've got to try a little kindness…..

Bobby Austin/Curt Sapaugh – Beechworth Music corp.

Some thoughts and musings can be a burden sometimes too, so be very gentle and kind to yourself along the way. Wherever you find yourself on your own pathway of discovery is quite okay. I was watching a *Songs of Praise* t.v. programme not long ago where a very wise man was asked what he did with the Big Questions of life. He answered so perfectly, "I live gently with them." Isn't that *sooo* lovely? **Live gently!** Later that night I was woken with thoughts about the simple statement and this poem found its way off my pen:

Live Gently

Questions so big I just

can't fathom.

A world full of strife, you can

never imagine.

A heart full of grief and

a pain so deep.

A mind so troubled, oh

where is sleep?

Catherine Grace

The answers are there,
but they just aren't yours.
They belong to the one who
sees it all!

So hang on to tomorrow,
you don't need to know.
Pray for the grace,
to let worries go!

Trust in the one whose
love is pure.
Strength will come,
yes – you will endure…

"…as you remember to live gently
with the big questions."
C.G. '23

Recently we were away on holidays and our very brave and wise Pastor preached a sermon on some of these big questions. It was wonderful that we were able to tune in to watch the service we were missing on Zoom t.v. If you are waiting for answers to some of these big questions and nothing seems to be coming, I hope this explanation from the Word brings hope to your day…

Gentle Whispers

But you must not forget this one thing, dear friends:
    A day is like a thousand years to the Lord,
    and a thousand years is like a day.
The Lord isn't really being slow about His promise,
    as some people think.
No, He is being patient for your sake.
He does not want anyone to be destroyed,
    but wants everyone to repent.
    2 Peter 3:8–10 NLT

In our fallen world, we will always hear of disturbing events. Some news seems too much to bear. We hear of things that are just unfathomable, and sometimes the Gentle Whisper may be for you to pray about something you don't even understand. So, my dear faithful friends… all I can say is **TRUST!** Trust the one who sees it all and knows the perfect way. Trust in His timing; trust in the outcome. Raise those holy hands to Heaven and believe in a brighter day and yes, **live gently!**

Gentle Whispers

Chapter Nine: In The Wee Small Hours

Silent night, Holy night,
all is calm, all is bright.
Round yon Virgin Mother and Child
Holy infant so tender and mild.
Sleep in Heavenly peace,
Sleep in Heavenly peace.

Joseph Mohr – 1816

These peaceful and beautiful lyrics were first written in Germany just after the end of the Napoleonic Wars by a young Austrian priest named Joseph Mohr. In the autumn of 1816, Mohr's congregation in the town of Mariapfarr was not happy at all. With war and the country's political and social unrest, this year was later known as "the year without a summer". Mohr's congregation was a very poor one and many were hungry and traumatised, so Mohr crafted a set of six poetic verses to help bring hope that there was still a God who cared for and loved them.

It wasn't until 1818, after Joseph Mohr was transferred to the parish of St Nicholas in Oberndorf, just south of Salzburg, that he asked his friend Franz Xaver Gruber, a local schoolteacher and organist, to write the music for his verses of peace and calm.

This carol certainly has been a wonderful gift to mankind, being sung for over 200 years every Christmas and often in between. Many school plays, choirs, and even well-known singers like Bing Crosby, Mariah Carey and Justin Bieber have recorded its melodic tune and restful lyrics. It certainly has brought sleep to me on many a restless night.

Are you one of those people who find sleep comes easily to them? My hubby's head hits the pillow and he is off with the fairies in no time at all. I, on the other hand, have a night pattern that goes something like this:

Gentle Whispers

Me: "Please let me sleep!"

Brain: "Lol, no, let's stay awake and remember all the wonderful and not-so-wonderful decisions you have made today!"

I know I am not alone with my day starting back to front. I wake up tired and I go to bed wide awake. Why does this happen, you ask? Ohhh, I wish I knew! Funnily enough though, my hubby will sleep like a baby through this whole episode of the lamp still on and me reading into the wee small hours. Sitting up in bed reading my devotional or a book is a good way for me to start this whole scenario, as long as it is a lovely story that won't bring visions of nasties and the need to solve the world's problems. Such is the dilemma of a deep thinker and creative phenotype!

There are many well-known people who don't, or haven't, needed a lot of sleep. Politician Margaret Thatcher; artist Leonardo da Vinci; company director Jack Dorsey; and inventor Thomas Edison all seemed to function well on three to four hours of sleep a night. It is interesting to note that research is finding more and more about our sleep patterns and has even found it may be a gene mutation that enables people to function well on fewer than six hours of sleep a night. Thank you so much, my dearly departed forebears!

An insomniac, on the other hand, is someone who experiences insomnia, the inability to fall asleep for an adequate amount of time. Although I don't put myself in this category, as I can fall asleep if the time and conditions are just right, my heart really does go out to those dear souls who find the necessary quantities of sleep impossible. If you are one of the 10% of the population who has this disorder, there is help available. There are many medical, holistic and natural remedies out there these days, and even apps on your phone that will play gentle waterfall music and other restful nature sounds to help you nod off into the world of rest, recovery and beautiful dreams. Sadly though, women of my age are best to stay away from any water or dripping sounds for obvious reasons! And don't forget those sheep. I hear the farmer still needs to know how many are up there in his back paddock! I do hope you will seek these out because if you don't, these fundamental processes are short-circuited, affecting our thinking, concentration, energy levels and moods. And who wants to be continually asked, "Well, who got out of the wrong side of the bed today?" or be found sleeping somewhere when they should be hard at work.

Remember this little fellow?

Little Boy Blue

Come blow your horn.

The sheep's in the meadow,

the cow's in the corn.

Where is the boy that looks after the sheep?

He's under the haystack, fast asleep.

Eugene Field – children's poet 2.11.1850 – 4.11.1895

Did you ever wonder if the sheep in this favourite children's nursery rhyme were supposed to be in the corn and the cows were meant to be in the meadow, but because Little Boy Blue had fallen asleep the naughty animals had run off into the wrong paddocks? After contemplating this dilemma, there are many and varied explanations for this rhyme, so I will let you make up your own mind as to what really did happen. The reason I have included it here though is because many and varied things are happening all around the world as we sleep. But firstly, I'll remind you of another rather sad story where sleep occurred at probably one of the most important times in history:

Then Jesus went with his disciples to a place called Gethsemane, and he said to them, "Sit here while I go over there and pray." He took Peter and the two sons of Zebedee along with him, and he began to be sorrowful and troubled. Then he said to them, "My soul is overwhelmed with sorrow to the point of death. Stay here and keep watch with me." Going on a little farther, he fell with his face to the ground and prayed, "My Father, if it is possible, may this cup be taken from me. Yet not as I will, but as you will." Then he returned to his disciples and found them sleeping.

Gentle Whispers

"Couldn't you men keep watch with me for one hour?" he asked Peter. "Watch and pray so that you will not fall into temptation. The spirit is willing but the flesh is weak."

Jesus went and prayed three times and then returned to the disciples, but on the third time he left them sleeping because their eyes were heavy.

Then he returned to the disciples and said to them,

"Are you still sleeping and resting? Look, the hour has come and the Son of Man is delivered into the hands of sinners."

Matthew 26: 36–45 NIV

I find this description of Jesus's last days so upsetting. How I wish the disciples had been able to stay awake to watch and pray. There certainly were enough serious and disturbing things to be praying about. I wonder if I would have been able to stay awake. Everything in me says I would, not only because of my devotion to Jesus, but for the fact he had asked me to. Maybe Luke's later explanation is correct, saying that the disciples were exhausted from sorrow, so maybe I would have been just like them. I often wonder if this played on the disciples' minds after the events following this dreadful night. Whatever the reasons, we do know it was part of God's perfect plan to save mankind, and Father God certainly was who Jesus needed that lonely night of grief and torment. His disciples would soon learn the significance of this night. Praise God for the deep trust Jesus had in His Father.

<u>*While You Are Sleeping*</u>

The story for this chapter isn't so much a story but something I hope you will think about. It is something that started happening to me quite a few years ago. I know I am not the only person in the world this happens to, as my eyes and ears have been opened to many other episodes I've read about or been told about since my first episode. I'm grateful confirmations have come along over the years to settle and confirm my inquisitive mind.

Do you ever remember your dreams? I usually don't. I will wake up knowing I have had a dream but can't, for the life of me, remember what it was about. Then, one night, something rather strange happened. It was a night when I was finding it hard to nod off into blissful sleep, but then I started to have what I can only call a half-asleep dream. When I woke, I could remember everything very clearly, but the astounding thing was the person in my dream was someone I had known when I was growing up. I had not had any contact with this person for at least fifty years, but there they were in my dream as clear as a bell.

The dream wasn't disturbing at all, but it left me lying there wondering what it was all about. How strange they would appear in my dream when I hadn't seen or even thought of them in all that time. I started to pray and asked the Lord to show me why the person would be in my dream. Then the thought came in the familiar Gentle Whisper: "Because I need you to pray for them."

So that is exactly what I did. I didn't know anything about this person now, or what they were doing, or where they even lived, but I definitely could pray for God to meet their every need; to keep them safe from all evil and harm; to heal their bodies from any infirmities; to fill them with His perfect love; and to save their souls. I just prayed whatever popped into my head. After this rather strange episode, I fell into a beautiful deep sleep, but I did remember all of it when I woke up in the morning.

From that experience and right up to now, I have given God permission to send these Gentle Whispers any night He needs me to pray for His precious children or any situation He knows needs His intervention. I've wondered long and hard about these episodes. Why not just pop the person's name into my head to pray for them; surely there is someone who knows them now who can pray for them; does the person even believe in God; couldn't God intervene anyway without my prayers; would the person even know who I am? Well, I know that no, they don't, because the people God has me praying for are many and varied, and sometimes even famous people from different parts of the world. The one common denominator though seems to be that I will recognise who they are.

I was encouraged a couple of years ago by a reading of declarations that included a page on dreaming:

DREAM

I declare that you will be an imagineer. I declare that you would not only dream but that you would have innovations in your dreaming. That you would create with a resourcefulness that not only brings joy to you but also joy to others. May your creativity not just be limited to the creation of art, but the merging of technology for the advancement of culture and society. May your ideas eradicate disease, solve political discord, improve quality of living. May your ideas excite you, sustain you financially, bless your family, your churches, your nation and even the nations. I command the voices of discouragement to silence themselves and I declare that downloads and strategies from Heaven would flow to your mind, hands and hearts.

Roma Waterman – Worship Leader; Songwriter; Author; Prophetic Voice

Book – Declare: Daily Declarations of Hope for the Modern Soul (2020)

This meaningful script certainly struck a chord with me. It was as if God was speaking with His Gentle Whispers directly to my own spirit, especially when it mentioned some of the traits I already had. I'm not sure I felt I was up to my art advancing society or my ideas changing nations, but sometimes we have to let go of who we thought we were to find out who we really are. Was I really a person whose life and dreams could be used in this way? The thought of being able to pray blessings, support and help into people's lives when they needed it most was simply a wonderful awareness that God could use even me, just as He is with many others around the world who pray in this way.

A very common question is: why does God need us to pray if He knows what we need anyway? Would you think less of me if I told you I don't really know? What I do know though is that God, in His most selfless act of love, gave us all a free will to live on this earth in whatever way we choose. He is never going to take that priceless gift away from us because it is impossible for God to change the character of who He is. HE IS GOD, the great I AM. What He does do is draw ever so close to us to bring about the changes He knows we so desperately need. One of the ways He is doing this is through the intercession and prayers of those He loves so much.

> *I urge, then, first of all*
>
> *that petitions, prayers, intercession*
>
> *and thanksgiving be made for all people –*
>
> *For kings and all those in authority,*
>
> *That we may live peaceful and quiet lives*
>
> *in all godliness and holiness.*
>
> *1 Timothy 2:1–2 NIV*

When we are asking God to intervene in someone's life, we are actually petitioning Him, requesting He meet the deepest needs of this precious person's life. Maybe they aren't asking for help themselves; maybe they don't think they deserve help; maybe they are too proud to reach out for help. Who knows? But I do know prayer is essential, and millions of people all over the world can testify to the fact their prayers have been answered; miracles have been at work; and the mysteries of God have been experienced.

Children are never too young to be learning and experiencing all that prayer can be in their lives too. I'm often horrified at what our young ones are exposed to in their everyday lives. The world they are growing up in is definitely different to the one you and I had the privilege of knowing. It really is such a shame children these days don't know the innocence and safety of playing outside with their friends until the streetlights come on, and then racing home in the dark, hoping you won't get scolded for being late. Television shows like *Lassie*, *Rin Tin Tin* and *Gidget* are a far cry from the superhero and often very violent ones of today. We still played innocent make-believe Cowboys and Indians, mothers and fathers, or fantasy games, which really are a far cry from the overstimulating and visually impactful games of today. I'm sure those fairies still live at the bottom of my garden. I enjoyed such a beautiful time with my grandson, whom I was privileged to mind weekly in his younger years, making a fanciful secret garden with little ornaments, shells and treasures we would find when fossicking around.

Gentle Whispers

A beautiful gift for my granddaughter from a caring aunty was one such garden. It was so sweet with cute little figurines and creatures hiding amongst the plants where her imagination could go to such beautiful and pretty places.

Friends, I'd say you'll do
best by filling your minds
and meditating on things
true, noble, reputable,
authentic, compelling,
gracious – the best, not the worst;
the beautiful, not the ugly;
things to praise, not things to curse.
Philippians 4:8 – The Message

Isn't it far better for our little ones' minds to be filled with things that create a positive and healthy mindset rather than things that fill them with fear and negativity? I know we can't wrap them up in cotton wool until they are old enough to fly the nest, but I do think it is a parent's responsibility to protect their children from harmful content that can cause such disturbances in their minds that lead to ongoing adverse problems in their future. As a parent myself, there were decisions we made that weren't very popular at the time. What child wants to be the only one amongst their school friends who wasn't allowed to watch a particular TV show, or wasn't allowed to own certain toys that really did belong to the dark side? Demonic forces are real, and we do need to give our children the tools to be aware and to be able to live life victoriously above such things without fear. Is filling their minds with scary, violent and disfigured monstrous images going to help them at all? All I can say is each parent has to make their own decisions as to what they believe is best for their child. Every family has different situations they are living in, and they certainly do have unique vulnerabilities from generations that have gone before. This is where having your heart and ears open to those Gentle Whispers is so important. God does know what is best for your precious children to have sweet dreams in the wee small hours and not be troubled by nightmares because of what they have been exposed to during the day.

According to the Australian Parenting Website, one of the main problems with this modern age is overstimulation of all the senses in our children, which happens when they are overwhelmed by more visual experiences, sensations, noises and activity than they can cope with. Action-themed cartoons, even though good usually overcomes evil, are often so graphic with gory details of these gross images that the child is left traumatised long after the movie is over. The danger here is that the child may not even verbalise their fear or understand it. Sadly, it will often show in other behavioural actions or emotions. It is well documented and researched by child psychologists and paediatricians that these exposures, which can cause emotional and mental disturbances, may last well into adult life with not only symptoms of anxiety and distress, but even domestic violence and other disorders including insomnia, eating disorders and aggressive or reclusive behaviour. It does make you wonder if all the video games children play on screens these days are one of the causes of so much violence and crime in our society today. They all move so fast and the volume button just has to be up. Goodness, have you been to the movie theatre lately? It is important to remember there is a dark side and it is real. It isn't to be afraid of because the good in people is more powerful than the bad, but it is not to be toyed with either or pushed aside as being harmless. Leave the dark side for God to deal with and choose for your children to live in light and love.

Little children,

you can be certain

that you belong to God

and

have conquered them (the evil one).

For the one who is living in you

is far greater than the one who is

Gentle Whispers

in the world.

1 John 4:4 TPT

This leads to the question: does all this darkness and negative imagery in so many of the movies and games today block out awareness of the 'unseen' heavenly world? It is worth thinking about. Of course, praying a covering over our young ones is so important. Their innocence seems to be stolen away from them at such an early age. Technology, in some ways, really hasn't done them any favours in the area of letting children be just children. Social media can be so damaging, with one post having the potential to ruin a pure and innocent soul! I'm very grateful and encouraged to know parents who are doing their best to address these damaging problems. It brings me hope, and to many other grandparents like myself. We never had to address the progress of mobile phones, video games, or the internet with its stalking, scams, hacking and bullying. Even G and PG movies these days seem more like M and M15+. Please know we are cheering you parents on with all our hearts and praying as we think of the future that lies ahead. That is something we can all do in the wee small hours. If we aren't having dreams or being prompted with others to pray for, we can certainly all be praying for our children, grandchildren, nieces, nephews, and the children in our neighbourhoods and local schools. They really do need all the prayer and support they can get, for they are the ones who will be running our world in the future. Oh, how wonderful for them to be able to hear those Gentle Whispers too, as they grow into the women and men God has created them to be.

I sincerely hope my, what may seem to be old-fashioned and fuddy-duddy words, have struck a chord with some of you. I am in awe of the amazing parents of today doing the very best they can with what they have. So maybe just do me a little favour and think about the above words, and just love me anyway!

I'm reminded of the simplicity of this poem that is a prayer:

Catherine Grace

Vespers

*Little Boy kneels at the foot of the bed,
droops on the little hands little gold head.
Hush! Hush! Whisper who dares!
Christopher Robin is saying his prayers.*

*God bless Mummy, I know that's right.
Wasn't it fun in the bath tonight?
The cold's so cold, and the hot's so hot.
Oh! God bless Daddy – I quite forgot.*

*If I open my fingers a little bit more,
I can see Nanny's dressing gown on the door.
It's a beautiful blue, but it hasn't a hood.
Oh God bless Nanny and make her good.*

*Mine has a hood, and I lie in bed,
and pull the hood right over my head.
I shut my eyes, and I curl up small,
and nobody knows that I'm there at all.*

*Oh! Thank you God for a lovely day,
and what was the other I had to say?
I said "Bless Daddy" so what can it be?
Oh! Now I remember it. God bless me.*

A. A. Milne, English writer, 18.1.1882 – 31.1.1956

Gentle Whispers

Of course, my favourite verse in this well-known, beautiful children's vesper by writer and poet A. A. Milne is "Oh! God bless Nanny and make her good." Do you ever wonder if Nanny was a tad naughty? How special is it to have children at an early age learn to pray and intercede for others? I do pray and hope your children are learning this way of life too. It can be confusing and a tad discouraging if they do not see their prayers answered in the way they would want, but I have always tried to explain that it is our job to pray the prayers and God's job to answer them in whatever way He knows is best at the time. Building trust into little hearts and minds is such an honour and an essential thing. I am reminded of the verses too that acknowledge the importance of a child's prayers, dreams and visions.

And afterward, I will pour out my Spirit

on all people.

Your sons and daughters will prophesy,

your old men will dream dreams,

your young men will see visions.

Joel 2:28 NIV

No one is left out here. All people; sons and daughters, old men and young men are all mentioned. But what about the old women and young women, I hear you ask? I try not to get too hung up on these issues. We are reading these verses from ancient times, when their religious, social and community rules were so different to how ours are today. Equality has come such a long way, hasn't it? Thank God! I am quite happy to include the old and young women in these verses and know that is how God sees it. He is the God of all things equal!

A beautiful memory I have of a very special moment is one of my eldest grandson, who was only three and a half at the time and who is now a teenager. Where did those years go is something I think every grandparent says. So was this a vision or a prophecy? I'll let you decide! The occasion was the launch of my first book. It is customary to have the author, or someone they choose, do a reading of excerpts from the book. I had decided I would prefer not to do the reading myself, so I wrote out a few paragraphs from each chapter and handed them to different willing people who were in attendance. The slip I had handed to my eldest son was quickly snatched out of his hand by my grandson, who was looking at it intently. Being three and a bit years of age, I knew he had no idea what the words said. Each person I had given a paragraph to read did so beautifully; I could not have read them better. Then it was my grandson's turn. I wasn't sure whether to ask him to hand the note back to his dad, but before I could do anything about it, he raised the paragraph up in front of his face, very seriously and with such confidence, and started 'reading' in a clear, loud voice, saying, "You should all read this book because it is very good!" You can imagine the reaction from everyone there. It was such a precious moment from someone who has gone on to do many moments of public speaking far beyond what you would expect from someone of his years. You know I'm going to say he certainly was having a Gentle Whisper to make his Granny's book launch just that extra bit special, don't you?

Something I am looking forward to knowing one day is whether the people who are in my dreams, and whom I have prayed for in the stillness of the night, have been helped and had their deepest needs met in some way. The reasons and ways the prayers are answered are up to God, the instigator of the request to pray for His dear child. I may not even find out this side of Heaven, but that is okay too. I will leave that all in God's sovereign will and just be grateful this little unknown somebody was given the privilege of being a part of the miracles of Gentle Whispers when the stars were shining brightly in the still of the night.

Prayer is a surge of the heart.

It is a simple look toward Heaven.

It is a cry of recognition and of love

embracing both trial and love.

St. Thérèse of Lisieux (2.1.1873 – 30.11.1897)

Gentle Whispers

Reflections: How are you going? I do hope this chapter is touching your heart. I did promise I wouldn't be too religious, as I prefer my writings to be more user-friendly and not too preachy teachy, so I hope the simple way of making sense of some of these topics is helping. I am well aware some of you are more advanced in the realms of the supernatural than I am, but I did want to try and at least explain in an easy way the fullness of the triune God and just how Gentle Whispers can come in the form of dreams. If you aren't already, I do hope you will be open to this concept and be amazed at how meaningful and helpful it is to those around you and the world in general. To be used in intercession in this way while you are sleeping is such a privilege and connects you to the awesome mysteries of God.

Maybe you aren't into the whole concept of dreams being used in this way at all, but that doesn't stop you from being able to put those sleepless hours to good use and start a prayer list for others. I'm sure those sheep could do with a break by now! There will be countless people in your life who could do with a little prayer – well, a lot of prayer actually. Before you know it, you will probably be off in the most peaceful sleep, and I know Heaven will not mind at all that you were in the middle of praying for little Johnny who needs to do well in his maths exam tomorrow when you finally do doze off. The most beautiful thing about that is that the Holy Spirit says He will finish the prayer for you. Do you believe this is possible? I do. It does say in the Bible, in Romans, that:

> *We do not know what to pray for,*
>
> *but the Spirit Himself intercedes*
>
> *for us through wordless groans.*
>
> *And He who searches our hearts knows*
>
> *the mind of the Spirit,*
>
> *because the Spirit intercedes for God's people*
>
> *in accordance with the will of God.*
>
> *Romans 8:26 NIV*

It also says in Hebrews that Jesus is interceding for us:

Therefore He is able, once and forever,

to save those who come to God through Him.

He lives forever to intercede with God

on their behalf.

He is the kind high priest we need,

because He is holy and blameless,

unstained by sin.

Hebrews 7:25 NLT

How blessed are we? It is so reassuring that when we don't know how to pray, the Holy Spirit and Jesus do, and oh, how our world needs these perfect and pure prayers.

Sadly, as the years roll on, man as a whole does seem to be more and more stubborn and further away from God. Do you ever wonder why? Maybe it's because they see the world becoming more evil, with sin and selfishness becoming more rampant. Man has always needed to blame someone, and often it is God! Maybe it's because they think God isn't doing enough, or doing things quickly enough, so they take matters into their own hands. Oh, why haven't they read the reading I quoted previously in 2 Peter 3:8–10?

I wonder if it could be the lack of understanding and disbelief that is holding it all up, or a refusal to be sorry and repent! Now, that is such an unpopular word today, isn't it – repent!? If only they could have faith to believe in the perfect outcome that is awaiting us all. It still does make me wonder though:

I wonder

There are many sounds that bring me comfort,

waves crashing on the shore are one.

Reminding me that I'm not in control…

No one is, since the world has begun.

Gentle Whispers

So why does man think he is so powerful?
He can't make the waves or moon or stars!
We are very good at making mayhem,
and causing pain with so many scars.

For me, God has always been easy to believe.
I find no fault in His ways or means...
How can I, when His world was made so perfect...
Such beauty that no eye has ever seen.

So why do we condemn Him when things go wrong?
I thought it was man who made all the harm!
And then we grumble, complain and need blame,
and carry on with such alarm!

I wonder the outcome if we'd all JUST PRAY...
Lay down our pride and humble our ways.
I wonder the difference if we'd keep the rules,
I'm sure we'd see much better days...
Do you ever wonder?
C. G. 2022

What a gracious and forgiving Heavenly Father He is; we do not deserve it! A wonderful prayer we can pray when the words won't come is The Lord's Prayer. Remembering Jesus intercedes for us at such times, I'm also so grateful Jesus gave this priceless prayer as a gift to us. Do you know it? Maybe your thoughts are going back to your early years in school when we would start the week by saying it at Assembly every Monday morning. My, how times have changed! When I was very young and attended Sunday school, it was one of the first Bible verses we had to learn off by heart. It is so lovely to have this prayer constantly in my mind. Well, sometimes in the back of my mind, which is absolutely fine, because at any of those times when my mind is in a muddle or overloaded, I can ask the Lord to bring it to the front of my thoughts and pray these beautiful words from Jesus. And He said unto them:

The Lord's Prayer

Our Father which art in heaven,

hallowed be thy name.

thy kingdom come.

thy will be done in earth as it is in Heaven.

Give us this day our daily bread,

and forgive us our trespasses

as we forgive those who trespass against us.

and lead us not into temptation,

but deliver us from evil.

For thine is the Kingdom,

The power and the glory,

Forever and ever, Amen.

Matthew 6:9–13 KJV

There have been many times over my life when the words just wouldn't come. As I've said, situations in life can be so overwhelming and traumatic that we just can't find the head-space to pray. The old original version above of the Lord's Prayer is what is etched on my mind from childhood, but there are so many new translations you may find more suitable if you don't already know this timeless prayer, like this one from the Good News Translation:

Gentle Whispers

The Lord's Prayer

Our Father in heaven:

may your holy name be honoured;

may your Kingdom come;

may your will be done

on earth as it is in heaven.

Give us today the food we need.

Forgive us the wrongs we have done,

as we forgive the wrongs that others

have done to us.

Do not bring us to hard testing,

but keep us safe from the evil one.

Amen.

Matthew 6:9–13 Good News Translation

I was so encouraged recently when we attended an Anzac service near where we live. We usually travel back to our hometown in the country where the brilliant autumn colours are always calling this time of year, but it wasn't possible with Anzac Day falling in the middle of a busy week. Instead, we took a ferry ride near our home across to the service there, which was in a beautiful waterfront Remembrance Park. The minister who was leading the service led everybody in a prayer – yes, The Lord's Prayer. There was a huge crowd at this service, all there to pay respect with grateful hearts, to remember those who had fought to save our country and give us a life of freedom and hope. Heads were bowed, and then a quiet murmur started to roll off the lips of all those attending. It was such a beautiful moment, and as the prayer continued, the murmur became louder as the crowds started remembering the familiar words. When the final amen was spoken, there was a tranquil hush, as if time was standing still for a moment. The thought came to me that it was probably years and years since some of these dear ones had prayed this prayer, maybe not since their childhood. I prayed then, requesting The Lord's Prayer would stay in these individuals' memory banks for moments when they would need to stop and reflect on their lives in the days to come.

So never fret when you can't pray. That is when you can put on your favourite worship music or go for a stroll to visit the ducks. Breathing in the beauty of nature is sometimes all you need to settle your heart and clear your head. A lovely cup of tea works wonders too, when you can quieten down with your favourite book, knowing your understanding, all-knowing Heavenly Father is not judging you but knows it is your time to receive some much-needed rest and prayer for yourself. He has it all under control and wraps it all up with His everlasting love that blankets you until the difficult reasons have passed.

Another reason we don't have to worry if the words won't come is because I do believe God places your name on someone else's mind to pray for you. It is so lovely to have someone come to you and ask, "Are you okay? You came to mind and I felt so strongly I was to pray for you." That is when you truly know Gentle Whispers have been at work. The person praying for you doesn't need to know your situation. God is such a trustworthy Father. He isn't going to disclose your deep secrets to anyone, but He is going to send the Holy Spirit with Gentle Whispers to pray Jesus into your situation to meet your every need, and yes, even in the middle of the night through dreams.

Lord, keep me safe this night,

secure from all my fears;

May angels guard me while I sleep

till morning light appears.

John Leland – Baptist Minister 14.5.1754 – 14.1.1841

So what is an ending?

Catherine Grace

From Beginning To End

"So what is an ending?
If you believe in eternity
there really is
no ending at all!"

C.G. '24

I hope the above quote excites you as much as it does me! To think we don't have to worry about 'the end' is quite liberating and freeing, don't you think? As far as this book goes, though, there will be a final page. You may feel some of my stories are a little far-fetched in how I have interpreted their circumstances. Well, that is quite okay too. We are all made so differently and uniquely, but what I am hoping with all my heart is that this will be the beginning, or the continuation, of knowing that, as you live each day, Gentle Whispers are being prepared for you right now. God desires so earnestly to communicate with His children. I'm so excited for you!

There are many people, probably even millions, who have heard from God during their lives. It doesn't matter if you are world-famous or just a humble member of the community like me, as God loves us all so deeply, equally and without any condemnation. The one thing He is waiting for, though, is whether you are listening. Are you available for the prompting that can only come from God when we are willing to be used by Him? So many people need intervention every day, and all that Heaven is waiting for is someone who will be available to be that help, give that encouraging word, show that love, and brighten that day. His surprises are so unique, many and varied. He is just waiting for the messenger.

We all have seasons in our lives when there just doesn't seem to be enough hours in the day to even stop and listen. I really do understand! This is where the Ecclesiastes 3 passage (back on page 98) can bring you hope. There **is** a time for everything. When I look back to the time when I had three children growing up and a husband who travelled for work, I wonder how on earth I got through each day. With getting them off to school, cleaning the house, washing the clothes, having meals ready, doing the shopping **and** running an art studio with everything ready for the next art lesson when I'd have eight ladies knocking on my door to be inspired, oh, I do wonder how I managed it all. But by the grace of God, and I only had three children! When school was finished, it was off to music practice, soccer practice, play dates, tennis matches, youth group, and shopping for their personal needs. My goodness, how fast they grow! Ohhh, and not to forget everything they needed for the next assignment that was due tomorrow! How many of you are hearing me right now and nodding your heads in agreement? Let me tell you, you are not alone, and all those who have been there, and all parents in the same position, are cheering you on! I am so grateful I had three amazing, helpful children and Jesus who was with me, enabling me every step of the way.

A beautiful actress, whose story I read recently, explains what it was like for her during these times while also having an acting career. Patricia (from *Everybody Loves Raymond*) explains she reconnected with her Christian faith during the beginning of the COVID-19 pandemic:

"There's a season of real busyness when you're raising children, having a family and working. Often, we don't make enough space to allow God to really talk to us. So I have more space now, and I'm hearing loud and clear!" she told *The Christian Post*.

One of the beautiful ways Patricia is doing this is by being an ambassador for World Vision, a Christian humanitarian charity lifting children, families, and communities out of poverty. How wonderful!

I know many of you will identify with all of this, but I want to encourage you again that in your busyness, maybe it is you who needs someone to pray for you, or someone willing to come across your path in response to a Gentle Whisper they have heard. We just have to graciously accept that help when it is offered. At times, it shows great strength of character and humility to admit we do need help along this often turbulent road called life. To be able to say we can't do it all by ourselves and a little heavenly intervention is really needed is such a beautiful thing. I believe that is when all the Angels rejoice and God, in His gracious wisdom and love, brings someone to rescue or encourage us. Often it will be from quite a surprising source. How wonderful to live with an expectant heart knowing there are faithful people out there ready and willing to respond to the Gentle Whispers!

So where do you think these Gentle Whispers come from? Who is the messenger from Heaven who delivers them to our ears and mind directly from God Himself? I believe it is God's third person, the Holy Spirit. From when I was a little girl growing up in a small religious country church, hearing of The Father, The Son and The Holy Spirit was familiar to me. But when praying, I would mostly start off with *Dear Lord Jesus* or *Dear Heavenly Father*. It was as if God was my Heavenly Father and Jesus was my best friend who lived in my heart and was with me every day, but The Holy Spirit didn't become 'real' to me until I was in my early thirties.

In some religions, parishioners will often cross themselves. A dutiful girlfriend of mine would often do this when needing help, especially if it was for a certain young, handsome boy to like her, or if she was facing an exam. Even though a little cheeky, I thought it was a special thing to do and admired her as such a good Christian. Because I wasn't of the same denomination, I thought I was not allowed to do it! It is the sign of the cross, and you will often see people of this religion crossing themselves when going into church. This wasn't a practice for our family, but we did respect that it is so important and meaningful for others. I can understand that for someone who wasn't church-raised at all, this can be quite a confusing idea. I remember when I first saw someone crossing themselves, I asked my Dad what it meant. He replied with tongue in cheek, "They are just showing they know where north, south, east and west is!"

In my first book, *Beauty All Around*, I try to introduce the hypothesis of beauty as the person of Jesus Christ. If you read between the lines, the short stories about life all describe a form of beauty that in reality would not have been possible if it weren't for the fact that Jesus is in my life and is in the beauty that is all around us. In Christian faith, this is well known. Jesus is beautiful because of who He is. Every single facet of

His character is gloriously beautiful, His holiness, pure heart, perfect love, joy, peace, kindness, humility, honesty, power, and a trillion other traits are what makes Jesus stunningly beautiful. The most beautiful of these is the sacrifice He made for you and me in dying on the cross to give us eternal life. If you don't have this belief, I pray with all my heart that one day you will know and accept the fullness of Jesus and the triune God into your heart.

Jesus' name above all names,

Beautiful Saviour,

Glorious Lord.

Emmanuel –

God is with us,

Blessed Redeemer,

Living Word.

Naida Hearn – 1974, Scripture in Song

In this book, *Gentle Whispers*, it has been my hope in introducing the fact that God does speak to us with these whispers that you will come to know just who The Holy Spirit is. I have already touched on this in Chapter Five, but I would like to share some more of my thoughts here before I go.

Theology teaches us the Holy Spirit is the third Person of the Trinity. He is co-equal with God the Father and God the Son, Jesus, and they are all distinct from one another in terms of their behaviour, functions and relationships. I am no great theologian, but in wanting to understand more about the workings of the Trinity, I try to think of it in the roles of my own life. Even though it may not be exactly correct, it does help me to understand. I shared these thoughts recently when a dear old soul I was visiting was struggling with how the Trinity works. This is what I shared with her:

I am Catherine, a daughter, a wife, and a mother. These are three different forms of me with three different roles, but I am still the one person. Each of these three roles I have will have me act, converse and relate to the others in different ways, but I am still the one me! I talk to my husband differently than how I speak to my son; I do things for my parents differently than the things I do for my children; and I talk and relate to my children differently than I do to my husband and my parents. They all know me as the one person, but I have different names and roles in each of their lives. All these three persons I am are still the one person, 'me', but I act appropriately and uniquely in each of my roles depending on which person I am.

That is the same as the Trinity: Father God, Jesus, and the Holy Spirit. All have their unique roles in my life. Of course, I do not dare compare myself to the Trinity of God in any way. The holiness and righteousness of God are incomparable. He is our everlasting Creator of all things and must be worshipped in spirit and in truth. I have just found this analogy, as imperfect as it is, helpful for me to understand the functions of God, and in doing so, my discernment in my Christian walk has become considerably more comprehensible and clear.

I would have to say, I really don't know how I managed this journey called life without the aid and intervention of the Holy Spirit at times. I received the Holy Spirit into my life the day I asked Jesus to be my Lord and Saviour. The Word confirms this, but I didn't really know how to apply His functions or His gifts in my life until I was in my thirties. What a wonderful day the revelation of this was!

In our world today, so much fear often infiltrates our minds, but the Holy Spirit brings such a deep sense of peace to my life and brings alive the perfect, all-consuming love that comes from the Father and Jesus to my heart and mind. The Holy Spirit is such a wonderful messenger and a gift Jesus gave to us with such love when He went to be with the Father. There is nothing more precious to me than that!

Such love has no fear,

Because perfect love

expels all fear.

If we are afraid

it is for fear of punishment,

Gentle Whispers

and this shows that we have not fully experienced His perfect love. We love each other because He first loved us.

1 John 4:18–19

One way we can show our love for others is to open up our whole being to receive those Gentle Whispers God so dearly loves to prompt us with. It really doesn't have to be complicated. Our minds are marvellous machines, really. I can see a gorgeous soft pink rose and lean in to smell its sweet perfume one day, and then on another day, when I see a beautiful rose, straight away I am reminded of a very special friend. It only takes a minute to then say a quick prayer for her, that God will send His Angels to protect her, that He will meet her every need and shower her with His love at that very moment.

You certainly don't have to be a 'holier-than-thou' person walking around with your mind in the clouds and being of no earthly good to anyone! Although, that being said, I'm sure God has a very special reason for some people being that way; I dare not judge! You may never know if your friend is in need of your prayers at that very moment, but chances are, if you have been prompted, then they definitely are. I am certainly not going to take the risk, as no prayer is ever wasted.

Another way is to pray a blessing over the person who has come to mind. How many times have you noticed someone and straight away thought how much they remind you of someone you know? This happened to me just recently. I was at a birthday lunch for a friend, and the sister of the birthday girl really could have been the twin of a lovely friend of mine I had not seen for many years. We did connect through social media sometimes, but the likeness was uncanny. All I could think to do at that moment was to pray a blessing in my mind over this friend. I later found out that she was travelling on the other side of the country, so who knows why she needed a blessing at that very moment.

Those details I can leave with a faithful God, and I can go about my day knowing that I have been part of what I believe could be a very special time for my friend, either in protection, provision, or even a promise fulfilled. I could have just shrugged that incident off as a mere life moment of two people looking alike, but how much better was it for me to have the privilege and joy of praying a blessing over my friend and being part of a God-surprise for her.

A favourite and very well-known blessing is this one, which is easy to learn off by heart:

The Lord bless you (put the person's name in)

And keep you.

The Lord make His face shine on you

And be gracious to you;

The Lord turn His face toward you

And give you peace.

Numbers 6:24 NIV

What a lovely way to be living one's life, open to the Gentle Whispers and promptings that are needed each day, at any given moment. You see, it's not complicated at all! Again, we may never know the outcome of our prayers or blessings. We may never find out why they were needed then and there. The joy is that we really don't need to know. We are just being part of the bigger picture, and the last thing God wants is for you to be bogged down with too much information and the burden of carrying all those worries that knowing too much can bring. Trust is the key, to leave the outcome to the One who knows and can solve it all. What better way to go about your day? We are thinking of and remembering people throughout our whole lives, so how very special it is to use those memories to say a prayer for them, then leave the outcome to God. That sure is a much better thing to do than to just have a passing memory moment and let it waft off into the breeze of nothingness. What a waste of time and space that would be. Can you imagine the difference in our world if we were all covering each other with prayers and blessings in this way?

Gentle Whispers

From the beginning of this book, tools have been shared on how you can be available to show your love for others by responding to the Gentle Whispers that have come into your thoughts. In summary, I suggest it may be to pray for a loved one who has lost their way, then reach out and knock on someone's door. Maybe you are on a journey of getting over those destructive feelings of low self-worth, so being able to encourage others with just how amazingly wonderful they are will surely help you both! Remember the chapter about my dear Dad? Is there someone you have to forgive? Oh Dad, I do love you and can't wait to live eternity with you, to experience completely the man God intended you to be, and the daughter God intended me to be too. I am grateful I did see snippets of it here, but to see my Dad and me completely healed will be an overwhelming joy I am so looking forward to. I wonder if I will even recognise the heavenly version of 'me'. Do you ever wonder this?

Forgiveness doesn't excuse

their actions.

Forgiveness stops their actions

from destroying your heart.

Anon.

Then there are those signs to look out for along the way. They do come in all different shapes and sizes, a truck on a highway, a babbling brook, and a caring friend who saw an ad in the paper were some of the signs God used along our journey. Yes, we do live in a fallen world, and bad things do happen to good people, but then a beautiful blue butterfly may just happen to flutter across your path too. For me, it was showing the importance of accepting the supernatural; the need to let go, to say goodbye, but to keep in mind that our lives are always changing, and peace will always come.

Gentle Whispers may come to you to support someone else in their time of waiting, or maybe you need to know your waiting time need not be wasted. And don't forget the importance of hearing and really listening to what those whispers are saying. When you listen intently, that is when you will be in the right place at the right time. Hearing and listening to what is being said through the wonderful sounds that may come through nature can be a revelation in itself. Spending time in the wonderful outdoors is so refreshing, as is reading and studying a daily devotional. I love what prophetic author Sarah Young says in her devotional *Jesus Calling*, firstly because she is speaking in the first person as Jesus. She explains:

"The Bible is the only infallible, inerrant

Word of God.

I endeavour to keep my writings consistent

with that unchanging standard.

I have written from the perspective of

Jesus speaking

To help readers feel more personally

connected to Him."

The devotion that followed really spoke to my heart:

As you listen to birds calling to one another, hear also My Love-Call to you. I speak to you continually, through sights, sounds, thoughts, impressions and Scriptures. There is no limit to the variety of ways I can communicate with you. Your part is to be attentive to My messages, in whatever form they come.

When you set out to find Me in a day, you discover that the world is vibrantly alive with My Presence. You can find Me not only in beauty and birdcalls, but also in tragedy and faces filled with grief. I can take the deepest sorrow and weave it into a pattern for good.

Search for Me and My messages as you go through this day. You will seek Me and find Me when you seek Me with your whole being.

Sarah Young – Thomas Nelson Publishers

Sometimes those signs and Gentle Whispers will come from a friend or a conversation with someone. God will even use circumstances and your thoughts, but never forget, they will come from God to you in whatever way He chooses. Are you listening? The Holy Spirit, who is the messenger Ruah, which in Hebrew means breath and wind, is longing to whisper so gently to your heart. I do hope you will let Him.

And lastly, to those dreams... to think your dreams can be used in such miraculous and amazing ways really is mind-blowing! We have no control over the visual imagery, thoughts, and dreams that come during those wee small hours, so doesn't it show us higher powers are at work? That really is all the more reason to give this time to God for Him to use in marvellous ways we could never think possible.

So why would we bother with all of this? Why even listen for the Gentle Whispers at all? Maybe you think that praying for and serving one another is enough. Of course it is, but wait, there is more. I'm sure you do know it is for LOVE. Yes, it's because of God's great and perfect love for us and because of the love we have for our fellow man that we should bother. It is also so we can see 'His Kingdom come on earth as it is in Heaven,' as the special prayer Jesus gave us says. What a privilege to actually be part of this powerful prayer, and what an honour it is to help someone in their life who really needs it, as I'm sure we all want a better life for those we love and for the world.

I have mentioned in some of the stories and thoughts in this book that Gentle Whispers aren't always to help other people, but are to bless us too. It's a sobering thought that we are able to bless others in our daily lives by following and acting on those thoughts and whispers that come our way, but how wonderful when it is us who are being blessed. Karma is alive and well in the universe, but I prefer to use the phrase, 'we reap what we sow.' Do you believe that? The more you respond to the Gentle Whispers, the more you will be the recipient of someone acting on those promptings to help you. That shouldn't be why you would want to help others, but for some mysterious reason, it is just the way the world goes around. The mysteries of God are a beautiful thing, a wonder to behold, and I do believe He yearns for us to pray. There are so many verses that tell us this:

"Always be joyful.

Never stop praying.

Catherine Grace

Be thankful in all circumstances,
for this is God's will for you
who belong to Christ Jesus."
1 Thessalonians 5:16–18 NLT

"Don't worry about anything,
instead pray about everything.
Tell God what you need
and thank Him for all He does."
Philippians 4:6 NLT

"Pray in the Spirit at all times and on every occasion.
Stay alert and be persistent in your prayers
for all believers everywhere.
And then the Apostle Paul continues…
And pray for me, too.
Ask God to give me the right words so I can
boldly explain God's mysterious plan
that the Good News is for
Jews and Gentiles alike."
Ephesians 6:18–20

Oh, I've just thought of something that happened to us recently, yes, just one last story to lighten the mood. Do you think you can cope?! It was a conversation my husband had with one of his work colleagues that tells of this very thing. Sometimes IT IS our turn to be blessed!

Gentle Whispers

<u>Tails that wag.</u>

A dog is a friend

who listens with his heart

and replies with his tail.

Anon.

Retirement age was quickly creeping up on us. I needed to face the fact that my art studio could be used in better ways than just two days a week for classes, so how about seven days a week, as a beautiful sunroom looking out to our pretty walled garden and courtyard? The thought of retiring was something we didn't entertain much. My husband was happy in his Property Manager job, and I was feeling very blessed with my studio running longer than I had ever thought possible! Twenty-two years blew my mind really, but I was four years past retirement age, and my husband was nearly seven! We threw ideas back and forth and thought we would just see how things rolled along.

A few of our friends were buying caravans, bigger cars to tow their caravans, and setting off on wonderful wild adventures to the outback and beyond. This never really appealed to either of us, plus there was no way we could afford it. My husband actually doesn't think caravans or campervans should be on the road, except at 1am in the morning! Are you shocked? Sorry, but with his car travelling for his previous job over the years to the back of beyond, he saw too many reasons to justify his opinion. Caravans trying to pass road trains are not a pretty sight, especially if you are the car coming toward them, or you are stuck behind a van travelling at 50 km/h in a 100 km/h zone with a very important appointment waiting for you. Well yes, it is very frustrating when there is nowhere to pass. Sorry if this offends anyone! As I've said before, just love him anyway, and I promise we will continue to pray for your safety on all your vanning adventures!

With many options coming to mind on how we would spend our latter years, it wasn't until a conversation with a work colleague that all became clearer. This lady didn't know she was saying anything so important to him; it was really just a passing comment in the middle of a conversation. We did, however, take her words as a Gentle Whisper meant directly for us, as it suited not only who we are but also what we love doing, which is exploring new places, being of help to people, travelling, and of course being in the company of cute little pets, especially dogs.

Research was started, enquiries were made, and soon we were proud members of Trusted House Sitters, an international group that allows hosts to go on their holidays with peace of mind, knowing their homes and precious pets would be cared for by a caring and competent sitter. Yes, that's us. We do love animals, especially dogs; we really love exploring new places; we love home living versus camping; we love gift-giving, and the opportunity to be a blessing to others. What a perfect plan for our future. If this sounds like you, why don't you give it a try? It is so much fun!

With our little Maggie finding her heavenly wings earlier in the year, it really was the right time to be able to help others in this way, by looking after their precious pooches and homes while they travelled to places far and wide. We have just finished our thirteenth sit, and the joy we have experienced during this time has been life-changing. We are welcomed into people's homes with open arms, and there is nothing more heart-warming than the love of a smoochie pooch who is so grateful for all the love and attention we can give them in return.

While the hosts are away on their holiday, we send them updates and photos of their fur babies living their best lives, as we have no trouble spoiling them. It is also an opportunity for us to look out for ways we can bless them on their return. We love leaving gifts behind and making sure the house is all clean and sparkling. We both love gardening, so pulling up a few weeds and mowing the lawn is always appreciated too. Gentle Whispers are much appreciated for this, as we pray and seek guidance as to what would suit each home best. It is interesting to note that we do not know much about the people we are house-sitting for. We don't really need to, as our job is to care for their pets and their home as if it were our own. But our Heavenly Father knows exactly what each home needs more than we do, so we wait on Him, and it

Gentle Whispers

doesn't take long before ideas spring to mind. How grateful we are for these Gentle Whispers.

It is so encouraging for us to receive appreciative feedback once the hosts are home. Really, it is the least we can do for being given the opportunity of being blessed with the company of precious pets while living in beautiful homes in places we had only dreamed about visiting and exploring one day. And, of course, there is a cherry on top to this story. The week my husband enquired about joining this group, he was told that if we joined that week, our name would go into a draw for lifelong membership, as there is a yearly membership fee to join. Well, of course, you know what I am going to say, don't you? Yes, we won lifelong membership! The call came from their London office in the middle of our grandson's Christmas concert. The lady on the other end of the phone could hear all the children singing in the background and asked in a very excited voice, "Oh, is that kookaburras I can hear?" That's a bit cute, isn't it? We are so very grateful! Why did we ever worry about what our retirement life would look like?

I'm not going to worry,

I'm not going to fret...

about all the things that

haven't happened yet.

He cares for the sparrows.

He cares for the trees,

so of course, He's going

to care for me!

The Lord is so faithful,

so kind and so true.

I'll wait for His whispers

to see me through.

C.G. '24

Some last little reflections: Maybe, though, because of deep hurts and the struggles of life, you have closed your mind to hearing from God at all. You certainly are not alone there. Many of us, including me, have tried to push God away at times. Where was He when I was hurting and in my darkest moments? Well, He was there, right with you, He promises never to leave you or turn away from you.

For God has said,
"I will never fail you.
I will never abandon you."
So we can say with confidence,
"The Lord is my helper,
So I will have no fear."
Hebrews 13:5 & 6 NLT

There are times when the dark clouds of sorrow are just too thick for you to be able to see through them. This fallen world can be very cruel at times. Sometimes it is from undeserved things that have happened to us, but it can also be our own sins that are sometimes too deep for us to want to see! And yes, sometimes our own choices, our free will, have put us in these places. At all these times, though, I have proved time and time again that God IS always there. If anyone has moved away, it is me, not Him. And all I have to do is gently whisper His name, and help is on the way. It may be a favourite song or verse that comes to mind. Your phone may ring, or there may be a knock on the door from someone who has heard those Gentle Whispers that you need a friend. I do hope this little book will help you trust again and let a glorious garden of peace and hope grow in your mind and heart once more.

<u>Whispering Hope</u>

Soft as the voice of an angel

Gentle Whispers

breathing a lesson unheard.

Hope, with a gentle persuasion,

whispers her comforting words.

Wait 'til the darkness is over,

wait 'til the tempest is done.

Hope for the sunshine tomorrow,

after the darkness is gone.

Whispering hope,

Oh, how welcome thy voice is,

making my heart

in its sorrow rejoice.

From Whispering Hope – sung by Jim Reeves

Written by Alice Hawthorne / Domenico Savino.

Bluewater music corp.

Now remember, it's not really the end! It's the beginning of a wonderful life ahead, where you will be experiencing the Gentle Whispers that have been especially selected for you to hear. And here is one for you to hear right now: "Ohhh, how perfectly loved you are!" Did you hear it?

Catherine Grace

Appreciations

There wouldn't be another book if it weren't for the gentle whispers God desires to give to His children every day. Thank You, Lord, for trusting me with these thoughts and for the ability to share them with others. Your perfect love and constant guidance and companionship are why I can get up every day. You are my everything!

I would love to acknowledge my supportive publisher, Sydney Book Publishers. The encouraging and professional team has been valuable in bringing my book to completion. I especially want to thank Jacob Baron and Oliver Brooks, Senior Book Consultants, who have worked tirelessly with such kindness and understanding in allowing me to be 'me' with my style of writing. Thank you to your editing team, who have shown such respect and patience in not changing my true stories and style, but have sprinkled them with the necessary grammar corrections here and there (it's a long time since I was in school, and my, how things have changed)! Oliver, thank you for your amazing knowledge of the industry and availability when we needed help. I do hope your bosses buy you a new coffee machine. You deserve it!

There have been people over the years, along with my family and friends, who have encouraged me with my writing. It took me many years to take notice, and it wasn't until a very loud prompting from Heaven that I actually did anything about this gift that I wasn't sure was to be made public. After writing courses to help spur me along, and my previous publications, there have been many of you who have encouraged me to continue writing my thoughts down. THANK YOU! I hope Gentle Whispers doesn't disappoint, as I do firmly believe God has very special words to say to each of you. You are so precious to Him, and He values and needs you in His world to make the differences that are so desperately needed.

I especially want to thank dear friends Val and Brian Stewart, who were my Pastors many years ago. Their wisdom, love, support, and friendship have lasted all these years, for which I am so grateful. Val Stewart OAM is a beautiful writer herself, along with holding many roles and gifts, including Pastor, Charity Manager, Public Speaker, teacher, mentor, and intercessor, to name a few. I have kept many of her beautiful words that she has written to me over the years, words that encourage, confirm, inspire, and give me confidence. They have been so important and appreciated. Val, your continued friendship and encouragement in my writings are greatly appreciated. And, congratulations on your new book, 'Heart to Heart'. I know it will bless all those who read it.

Another dear friend I want to acknowledge is Jenny, who was given my first book by her daughter. She wanted to have contact with me to thank me for my words that spoke to her heart, so she reached out. We have remained pen friends, which I appreciate so much. Jenny is always encouraging me by sending snippets she has read that she knows I will enjoy and gain inspiration from. Thank you, Jenny, you are a special gift from above whom I treasure.

I am also grateful for Robyn, who, without knowing me very well, was willing to be my Alpha Reader. Your encouragement, kind words, and assurance that the manuscript flows and makes sense, and that the content was helpful and believable, have helped me to continue to this last stage! Thank you!

Lastly, where would I be without my man! Graeme, you put up with my many requests for help, my 'untechno' brain, and my 'should I, could I, will I; and maybe I won'ts' over this last year, yet you are always so willing to come to my aid. Nothing is too much trouble, and I appreciate the many times you have read and re-read my words when asked. Thank you for believing in me and this project, and for allowing me to share some of your stories! Love you heaps!

Catherine Grace

About The Author

Catherine (or Cathy, as she is known to her family and friends) is married to Graeme, has three adult children with their partners, and three grandchildren. She lives on the picturesque Central Coast of N.S.W.

A work history in Decorative Art and High Tea now brings Cathy to retirement and more time for writing, which to date has included a book, three short stories, and published poems. She has won an award in the International Book Awards, has been successful in writing competitions, and is currently excited about her second book.

Cathy has also worked in Chaplaincy and Pastoral Care visitation in hospitals and aged care homes. She loves to bring Jesus, His companionship, love, and gentleness, into people's lives, which is where her writing style comes from. It's as if she is sitting with you, sharing stories over a lovely cuppa tea.

Her new book, *Gentle Whispers*, is a collection of true stories with thoughts and devotional reflections. It is her prayer that you will grow closer to God as you learn to listen for His Gentle Whispers.

Gentle Whispers

As we go to print, our world has changed, but light will always overcome the darkness-

It's early morning. I can hear the sweet birdsong and see the first hint of light. Sleep has not come easy these last few nights. Our computer is down just as the last format is being completed for this book. It's frustrating to say the least, but could it be for a reason? So my question in this stillness is "why God? We are almost completed"? Then the gentle whisper "because I need these words written".

In an instant, darkness has overtaken our country. This ugly season has been brewing for a few years now, but in a split second the worst act of terror and evil has just happened. 15 innocent people at a Jewish Hanukkah celebration have been senselessly killed. The world is screaming why? The reason is we are in a season of deep evil and darkness in our world. The prince of darkness, Satan is having his way through wicked men's freewill, to reject God and His way. God has not caused this evil, but there is hope. When darkness rules, God, in His mercy will always bring the most glorious and powerful weapon, LIGHT!

The light shines in the darkness

and the darkness can never

extinguished it.

John 1:5 NLT

God's plan is always to bring light, through His perfect love, healing and hope. In this instance also through heroes. There were many, but one hero was a man of Muslim faith who unbelievably ran in, risking his own life, to save many lives of the Jewish people who were being gunned down. I believe God's purpose in this dark time is to not waste one drop of the sacrificial blood that was shed this horrific day. Already we have witnessed Muslims, Jews, Christians, people of all faiths and people with no faith, come together in acts of selfless love, compassion and already forgiveness. Humanity is shining in its darkest hour.

Catherine Grace

Jesus spoke to the people saying,

> *"If you follow me, you won't have to walk in darkness because you will have the light that leads to life."*
> *John 8:12 NLT*

WILL YOU FOLLOW THE LIGHT?

www.ingramcontent.com/pod-product-compliance
Lightning Source LLC
Chambersburg PA
CBHW042114100526
44587CB00025B/4055